# FAMILY DAY CARE

# Family Day Care

## How to Provide It In Your Home

Betsy Squibb

The Harvard Common Press

The Harvard Common Press, Inc.
The Common
Harvard, Massachusetts 01451

Distributed by Independent Publishers Group
14 Vanderventer Avenue
Port Washington, New York 11050

© 1976, 1980 by Betsy Squibb. The writing of this book was funded
in part by the National Association for the Education of Young
Children through a Membership Action Grant. The opinions
expressed herein are those of the author and do not necessarily
reflect those of that organization.

Printed in the United States of America

**Library of Congress Cataloging in Publication Data**

Squibb, Betsy.
  Family day care.

  Bibliography: p.
  Includes index.
  1. Day care centers—United States. I. Title.
HV854.S68        362.7'1        79-12969
ISBN 0-916782-14-X
ISBN 0-916782-13-1 pbk.

Illustrations by Johanna Wagner

10  9  8  7  6  5  4  3  2  1

# CONTENTS

# INTRODUCTION

FAMILY DAY CARE is the oldest form of child care outside the home; it has existed for as long as children have needed to be cared for by people other than their own families. Simply stated, family day care is the care of a child in the home of another family for any part of the 24-hour day.

Such care may be part-time or full-time. It may include children from infancy through adolescence. It is as flexible and personal a form of child care as the people who provide it; and more and more it is being recognized as one of the best forms of care available for children outside their homes. Surveys show that as many as 80 percent of children in day care are in family day care homes.

There are good reasons for this trend. Family day care, it is clear, provides many advantages to all who are involved —the child, the parent, and the provider.

*1*

The group in a family day care home is small—state laws usually limit the number of children cared for to six. The child being cared for, then, is part of an intimate social setting, and has individual attention given to his needs. His sense of who he is develops as it would in his own family, naturally and spontaneously.

The child in a family day care home relates primarily to one adult. Just as in his own family, he can develop a trusting, caring relationship with his caregiver—a relationship that can provide continuity and stability in his life. When relatives and friends of the day care family visit, the child can learn to know them and be with them just as he would in his real family.

There is a very special relaxed quality to the way a child relates to the other children and the day care provider in a private home. Often the group in the home will include children of different ages, and so the child in care can learn to be with children who are at different stages of development from his own. An only child learns what it is like to have brothers and sisters. An oldest child finds out what it is like to be bossed around by bigger children; and the youngest child in a family can experience being looked up to by smaller children. In addition, because the group in a family day care home is multi-aged, brothers and sisters can be cared for within the same small group—an important factor in strengthening family life.

Parents as well as children often find their needs best served by the family day care home. For one thing, such care is usually provided by persons who live in the community where the parents live or work. As well, day care homes are usually flexible in their operating hours. If the parent's work schedule changes, the hours of child care can change more easily than they might in an institutional setting.

In a time when parents must make a tremendous effort to find suitable child care, the family day care home can offer an excellent solution. Parents and provider can develop a strong, stable relationship as joint caregivers to the child. The relaxed atmosphere of the home encourages this relationship to be personal as well as professional, and makes it easier for them to work together in dealing with individual child care situations.

Finally, the provider of family day care can meet some of her own important needs by supplying child care in her own home. She can put her skills as a nurturer to work for a professional purpose, without giving up her independence, flexibility, or control. Many providers start family day care homes in order to spend time at home with their own children while they continue to bring in additional income.

In addition, the skills developed by providing family day care are highly professional ones. Working with parents and learning to deal with their varying ideas and values requires strong human relations skills. And becoming familiar with child care resources and community services is an important part of the provider's job.

There are different types of family day care arrangements to consider when deciding to provide such a service in your community. Many providers operate on an *independent* basis. On their own, they set up their houses for child care, obtain the license to operate, arrange with families to provide care, and take care of the many details that running a family day care home entails.

Some providers, however, choose to be part of a family day care *system*. This is a network of family day care homes that operates under the supervision of a central administration—such as a private social agency, a day care center, or a community action program. The central agency usually provides help in getting started—including training for providers, help with licensing, referral of children and families, and general information. The system also helps with the administrative operation of a day care home, usually paying the provider a salary rather than having parents give fees directly to the provider. If you are interested in what a system might offer, ask the person responsible for licensing day care in your area for the names and addresses of systems near you.

Often independent providers will form an informal network of family day care homes, called a family day care *association*. Associations are formed mainly as support groups for individual providers; they can be an important force in breaking down the isolation that arises when you care for young children alone in your home. Through an association, independent providers can get together to work with children, families, and the community. They can also use their collective influence to work towards solving the professional problems—educational, legal, and political— of the family day care provider.

This book aims, above all, to share ways in which family day care might be made a richer experience for providers and children alike. Though it would be impossible to include every bit of the information and know-how necessary to provide family day care, this is not a real problem. For the providers of such care are their own most valuable resources—their own information is virtually limitless. Many of the ideas in this book are ones that providers have tried and found helpful. They should serve as a starting point for you and other family day care providers so that you may explore and share with each other the many resources you have, within your communities and within yourselves.

# 1.  LICENSING AND REGISTRATION

## FAMILY DAY CARE AND THE LAW

Family day care is legally defined as the care of up to six children (including the provider's own) in a private residence during all or part of the day.

There is a big difference between being a babysitter and providing family day care. Babysitters might take care of a child for a few hours while his parents are away. But a person who cares for children on a regular basis in her own home, either part- or full-time, for up to five days a week, certainly plays a large part in the development of those children, and deserves to be called something other than a babysitter. Family day care providers are different from babysitters in another important way: since they represent the parent, they are often called on to make decisions that the parent would usually make—such as meal planning, discipline, and even choices of learning activities.

Because family day care is considered to be such an important factor in the welfare of our children, it is regulated by law in almost all states. Most people are surprised to learn that a license is required for conducting a home business involving the supervision of young children. Why do regulations for licensing and registration of family day care homes exist?

Someone who cares for children unrelated to her in her home is, in fact, providing a public service. This public service, like any other, is subject to state regulation, which aims to assure that a service meets certain basic standards. The minimum requirements formulated by the agency that regulates family day care in your state are intended:

1. To prevent health or safety hazards from existing in day care homes.
2. To make sure that children in day care homes are not harmed physically or emotionally, so that they have a chance to grow and develop in a healthy way.

Many family day care providers give children top-quality care that is far above these minimum requirements. But the regulations are one way of recognizing the importance of the services these people provide. It's about time that the thousands of family day care providers in every state start getting some credit for the work they've been doing. Caring for children is an exciting job, but it is demanding, even if you love children.

## HOW TO GET LICENSED OR REGISTERED

There are different ways in which to get an "okay" from the state to provide family day care. The two main methods of family day care regulation are *licensing* and *registration*. (Registration is simply a new system of licensing, being tried by a few states.) In both these methods, the family day care provider checks with the state agency to see if the minimum standards are being met. If all conditions are met, then a license or certificate is issued.

In most states, the department of public welfare has responsibility for licensing family day care homes. In some states (Arizona, the District of Columbia, Maryland, and New Mexico, for example), licensing is done by the department of public health. A few states have special offices that coordinate children's services (the Massachusetts Office for Children, the Vermont Office of Child Development), and these offices will license day care homes.

Requirements for licensing or registration vary from state to state and even from county to county. The local social service agency, welfare department, or health department can give you complete details. However, here are some of the requirements you will need to meet:

1. You will be asked to fill out an application (or self-evaluation form). There will be questions about your home (toys, napping space, and the like), about you, your experience with children, and your family. You will also be asked to list at least two character references, people who can recommend you as a giver of family day care.
2. A doctor must fill out medical forms for you (and often for other members of your family) to show that you are in sound physical and mental health.
3. You will need to have a tuberculosis X-ray or skin test for yourself and everyone in your home over the age of sixteen. (Most persons working with children are required to have a T.B. test.)
4. The licensing worker will visit and inspect your home, and will talk with you about caring for children.
5. A health department worker will inspect your home, checking for fire hazards, wiring, plumbing, and soundness of construction, to make sure you are providing a safe environment for children.

In many states, the licensing/registration process is free. Others charge a small fee at the time of licensing and again each time the license is renewed, which in most states is every year.

The licensing/registration process may be completed as quickly as the necessary forms are returned and the inspections or visits are carried out. But arranging the required inspections or visits often takes longer than you think. Plan on a number of weeks for the process of becoming licensed or registered to be finished.

## THE BENEFITS TO YOU

Some state offices offer helpful services to registered or licensed providers of family day care. Such services can include:

1. An informal referral service to provide names of licensed/registered persons to those seeking family day care. A provider may decide whether or not to be included in this listing. It is important to note that the state licensing agency does not actually place children in homes.
2. An informal association of family day care providers. Some associations are statewide, others are county associations, and there are also associations in some larger cities.
3. Frequent mailings of helpful information, such as play ideas, free materials, and nutrition ideas; or information on workshops, courses, and general meetings of family day care persons in your area.
4. Consultation and help with issues of family day care.

## 2. A NATURAL LEARNING PLACE

YOUNG CHILDREN learn most effectively through their "work"—through *doing* things. There are many opportunities for children in the home to take part in the sort of real-life activities that adults and children do every day. These might include cleaning the house, making beds, doing dishes, preparing meals, shopping, growing things, fixing things, and so on.

Young children watch adults do these things and, by watching, they learn how to do them. If they participate in the doing with you, the activity becomes even more meaningful. It may even cut your time doing chores, after they get the hang of being helpful.

An important thing to remember is that little helpers can do a good job and do it happily if it is a job that they can successfully complete. Start with very small, easily accomplished tasks, and give "plenty of praise and mighty little criticism!" one provider warns. Don't expect perfection—"If you do, don't try it," she continues. "The kids haven't been at this as long as you and don't have the experience yet."

Infants don't really have to be excluded. They can watch from a nearby playpen, seat, or stroller, and see what happens. Or, how about giving the baby a household tool to touch and explore (plastic spatula, wooden spoon, soft cloth, etc.)? A lot of infants' learning is through feeling— they can learn about your work utensils by watching you and touching the tools.

Toddlers really are fun to have as helpers. They are very much caught up in the movement of cleaning and will walk around gaily waving their dustcloths in the air. They can help pick up and put things back, if you tell them where. Toddlers are learning what things are and where they belong by doing this. They are especially good at putting things in paper bags and closets, although they might take them out again, too, just to see what it's like.

## HOME ACTIVITIES CHILDREN CAN HELP WITH

**Dusting and picking up.** Little hands will eagerly dust off furniture. They will pick up and put back too, especially if you make a game of it. How about a bag or a carton with a picture glued on depicting the sorts of objects that belong in there (dolls, games, paper, etc.)? This is a good matching game.

The picking up that occurs after eating or after an activity is an important part of the experience. (Look in the library for a great book called *The Man Who Never Washed His Dishes,* by Phyllis Krasilovsky [Doubleday & Company, New York, 1970], which you can read to the children.) Cleaning up and putting things away gives us a sense of orderliness and knowing where things can be found.

An adult certainly can't expect a child *always* to pick up after himself—it's a habit we all have to acquire, unfortunately. A lot of praise and making the activity gay (singing what you are doing, or a song like "Whistle While You Work") helps it go better.

**Sorting laundry.** This is a good way to learn colors, textures, and how to put things in different categories, as well as how to follow directions. Mrs. H. has a left pile of white laundry and a right pile of colored laundry. Everyone stands around in a circle and decides what goes in what pile, and why. The older preschoolers enjoy this. They also like to count how many items are in each pile.

**Washing.** Washing dishes is ideal, both because it involves helping and because it is a good excuse for working with water—a favorite pastime for children.

If you have nonbreakable pots and pans and tablewear, there is no cause for worrying about breakage. You may find that it takes a long time to help wash, since it is so much fun. Handling the slippery dishes helps a child develop eye-hand coordination—the eye has to watch and control what the hand is doing.

Little hands can help dry the dishes too—an activity that requires concentration and using small muscle skills.

With a sponge, rags, and a small dish of soapy water, the children can help mop and scrub woodwork, counters, floors, or chairs. Show them how to wring out the sponge and rags, how to scrub and rub, how to mop up spills, and the washing will be easier for you and a learning experience for them.

House painting with water can be a form of both washing and painting. All you need is some water in buckets, and some different-sized paint brushes. On a sunny day you can paint the outside of a house, a play-house, an outside shed, a wall, or even the sidewalk. On a cold winter's day, you can paint windows and woodwork. Just spread plastic drop cloths under the area to be "painted," and maybe supply some painter hats.

**Sweeping and vacuuming.** These are good activities for using some of that energy (especially on a rainy or snowy day). You can use child-sized brooms (they might also be used for dramatic play) or you can make a small broom by cutting off the handle of an adult-sized broom. (Be sure to sand the edges.) It takes some coordination to learn to sweep dirt into a pile and then to pick it up. With a little patience from both of you, the dirt will make it to the right place.

The vacuum cleaner is a very noisy and mysterious machine for young children. It may be frightening for some of them at first. Try to explain how it works and where the dirt goes. It's fun for toddlers to turn it on and off, and they love to "help push." The preschoolers can help run it; try the small furniture nozzle at first, as it is more manageable.

Cleaning gives the young child a sense of responsibility and importance, and helps him develop into a competent adult.

**Setting the table.** This is especially popular with the three-, four-, and five-year-olds; they learn what utensils are needed in order to eat the food. Ask them, "What do we need if we are having soup to eat?" or, "How many glasses, plates, spoons, napkins, etc., do we need today?" This is learning in a practical manner how to count and to solve problems.

Help them figure out how to find things they might need. One family day care provider has cut out pictures of household objects from magazines and pasted them on the drawers or cupboards where the objects are to be found. The children can go looking and then discover where the things are kept. Later on, the written word of the object will be added under the picture. This is a good pre-reading experience.

**Building and fixing things.** Little helpers while you build are learning a lot about how things work. They can watch, hold tools for you, and help measure. Or, they can hammer on a board alongside you as you work. Help them learn about the tools (their names, what they do, what they are made of).

There is a type of heavy cardboard called Triwall, which you can use to build all kinds of inexpensive equipment for your home (cubbies, sand-tables, tables, storage, and such). For suggestions of things to build from Triwall, write to the Workshop for Learning Things, 3 Bridge Street, Newton, Massachusetts.

When the electrician, plumber, or telephone man comes to fix things, there are always a lot of interested little people right under his feet. It is important to explain what is being done and why. Fixers in the home provide an excellent opportunity for young children to learn about different trades and the work involved (the plumber works with pipes, the electrician works with wires, and so on). Watching someone fix something is good for enlarging their concentration spans. Also, it is exciting when someone new to watch and talk with is in the home.

**Growing things.** Whether it's inside or outside, children really love to watch things grow and find out about natural science. They can learn to water house plants and in doing this learn about the different needs of various plants. Some need water every day and some only once in a while.

An outside garden requires planning, and the children can help. Mixing the soil, testing it with litmus paper to determine acidity, finding and buying seeds— there are lots of decisions and things to do. Some questions to be answered would be: "Where can we find seeds?"; "What do we want to grow? Fruits? Vegetables? Flowers?"; "What makes these things grow?" The project can go in any direction and can involve a limitless number of questions, activities, and trips.

How about a winter garden? With a sunny window and a little luck, children can grow delicious vegetables indoors in the winter. Lettuce, sugar peas, even cherry tomatoes can be grown, brightening up drab winter days with color and providing wonderful snacks and salads.

To plant, just get some potting soil, put it in small

flower pots, paper cups, cut-up quart milk cartons, or any other convenient holder that is at least 2½ inches deep and has drainage holes at the bottom. Plant several seeds per container and then put them into drainage-catching trays made from half-gallon milk containers cut horizontally. Place these trays in a window.

Plants that produce fruit (tomatoes, peas, etc.) should be in direct sun much of the day. Lettuce, chard, beets, and carrots can go in a window that gets strong light but not necessarily direct sun. Keep the seedlings moist, but not too wet.

When the seedlings have produced six leaves, transplant them into pots at least six inches deep and feed them every two weeks with fish emulsion (fish nutrients). If you are growing tomatoes, keep the plants next to each other so they will cross-pollinate. If growing sugar peas is your thing, make a string trellis for them to climb.

One family day care provider planted with the kids at her house, and then went to Grandpa's garden to transplant the seedlings. All summer they would go over to help Grandpa water and tend the plants. This was a good way to combine gardening and seeing Grandpa work in his garden.

Some simpler gardening involves cultivating roots and stems from vegetables and fruits. Many vegetable and fruit seeds will grow if placed in water until roots develop, and then they can be transplanted into larger pots. These include carrot tops, pineapple tops, citrus seeds (grapefruit, oranges, lemons), and some pits from peaches, plums, and prunes.

How about growing a leafy potato plant? Put three toothpicks into the middle of a sweet potato or yam and place it in a jar of water. After a few weeks the potato will grow stems and roots. It can be transplanted into a large pot and will grow into a large, leafy plant.

An avocado makes a good plant. Plant an avocado seed in water with three toothpicks stuck in the sides to hold it up in the jar. Put it in a sunny window. After a couple of weeks, stems and roots will grow. One family day care provider says that she had to try this a few times before she had a two-foot-high beauty of a plant.

"Midget" or "Burpee" brands of seeds are good bets with children and can be found at nurseries or ordered from seed catalogues. And the pictures in seed catalogues are great for cutting out and pasting after you have ordered your seeds. With the pictures and some children's drawings, you can make a book about flowers or vegetables that you have grown.

A free book is put out by Chevron Chemical Company giving detailed suggestions for gardening indoors and outdoors. If you want to introduce your children to the joys of plants and need some hints, write to Chevron, Public Relations, 200 Bush Street, San Francisco, California 94120, and ask for a copy of "A Child's Garden."

## HOME LEARNING IN UNEXPECTED WAYS

A lot of learning is happening all day, every day, in the home—though it is not always planned. As you walk into the living room you might straighten a picture on the wall. A child will ask about what the picture is. You can talk about why people hang pictures in houses, what kind of different pictures there are, what the picture looks like— even what it looks like upside down or sideways as well as right-side-up. A young child is curious, and a home gives a lot of opportunities to examine things in a natural environment.

Or, a four-year-old might help a toddler push a wagon. When you ask the older child not to push too fast because the toddler can't walk as well on his unsteady legs, the four-year-old learns more about toddlers. He also feels important, looking out for the little guy.

Even minor disasters can provide learning experiences. One family day care provider found her drainpipe filled with ice one cold day and needed to unplug it. The five-year-old helped her put a snake through the frozen slush while the younger children watched. The provider talked with the children about how water freezes when it gets cold, and about how ice can clog up pipes, rivers, roads, and the like. She hadn't planned on having a frozen pipe, but the learning that occurred because of it will be important for the children in their own lives.

## LEARNING SOCIAL CONCEPTS IN THE HOME

Have you ever thought about how many different roles you show the children during the course of one day? You are a housekeeper, a mother, a cook, a shopper, a gardener, a nurse, a neighbor, a teacher—to name only a few. As the children observe you and imitate the many roles you show them, they understand their world better.

The home environment promotes independence in many small ways each day. Free access to the toilet when they need to go helps develop self-reliance in children. Being able to turn on faucets and pour and fill cups and containers all by themselves is a really good activity for fostering independence and responsibility.

In a family day care home, a child finds a nurturing environment that is unique. He has the opportunity to experience many important things: tender, loving care from an adult, respect as an individual in a group, meaningful relationships with adults and with other children, an informal environment with familiar routines that help order his world, and a variety of things to do that are stimulating and fun.

Homes don't have to fabricate realistic experiences for children the way schools sometimes do—because the experiences are already there in a natural state. Learning possibilities are endless in a home. Children pick up on this and adults can too. The excitement they share in discovering the possibilities in ordinary things is really contagious!

## 3.  THINGS TO DO

AS A CHILD GROWS, he matures and learns. During the first years, a child develops by leaps and bounds; he is learning at least as fast as his body is growing. He is learning about the world and working through his relationship with it.

Family day care providers facilitate the child's learning in a variety of ways. In the home, the child can learn and grow at his own pace and according to his individual needs. A caring adult can offer appropriate materials and activities to make learning meaningful at each stage of a child's development.

## THE RIGHT TOY AT THE RIGHT TIME

Children at different stages of development approach the same activity differently. For example, take a box and place in it assorted objects, such as different pots, pans, or utensils:

• The baby or toddler likes to move things in and out of the box; he is learning to handle various objects. Ask him, "What is this?"

• The three-year-old will identify two similar objects; he learns to recognize them by size and shape. Ask him, "What is this? What shape is it? Is it big? Small?"

• The four-year-old will identify two similar objects; he learns to arrange them first by their use, and then by their make-up. Ask him, "What is this? Is it for cooking? Sewing? Building? What is it made of? Plastic? Metal? Wood? Is it different from that one? How? Do you know what color it is?"

Almost any material can be a learning experience for a child. Materials have properties like weight, size, volume, and texture for a child to learn about—things an adult sometimes takes for granted. Kids often drop hints about what is too hard or too easy for them; the trick is to watch and to listen.

For the child, every sense can be used to learn new things. This is how the child will acquire skills, learn to make choices, and grow in ability and competence.

## ACTIVITIES FOR INFANTS

A play world exists everywhere, even within the confines of a crib. An infant does a lot of *looking at things* in order to see and to find out about his world.

• A reflective object such as a plastic mirror will delight a baby. Or, look with him in the bathroom mirror.

• A mobile with shiny objects or pieces of brightly-colored flannel on a hanger is nice to look at. Before you hang it up, look at it from a lying-down position to see it the way a baby would see it.

● A string of beads can be stretched across the crib—how about letting a four-year-old string them for the baby?

● A cradle gym is very useful. After looking at it for a while, or hitting or kicking it, the baby may pull himself up with it. You can make a cradle gym with a string and a piece of rubber hosing; put the string through the tube and tie the string to each side of the crib. Then hang things from the tube, such as spools, beads, or bells.

● Your face is important to him—babies love to be smiled at, talked to, and sung to.

Infants like to *grasp things* and learn that they can make something happen to objects. Such action objects could include:

● Rattles
● Plastic nesting cups, which a baby can take apart and put together later on
● Squeeze toys that make noises and give him a sense of power because he's making a sound
● Soft stuffed animals to touch
● "Feely" toys with interesting textures
● Empty orange juice cans to roll and try to catch
● Small balls that roll.

Infants will listen to sounds and try to sort out what makes what sound. Bells, which can be tied or sewn to booties or socks, or things that swing against each other, make interesting sounds for a baby. Babies will also enjoy soft music on a record player or the radio; singing by you or other children; or music boxes.

Infants are learning to respond to other people. There are some simple *games* you can play with a baby:

● Peek-a-boo
● Singing pat-a-cake and clapping hands
● Imitating sounds the baby makes and responding with surprise as he imitates you.

A baby of eight months or so will begin to make his own games. It helps him if you enlarge his possibilities. Put toys within reach—he will start to grasp and throw things. Throwing a rattle on the floor is a favorite for babies—you will get tired of it long before they do!

Around the age of twelve to fifteen months babies love to fill and empty things. A large milk carton cut in half makes a fine bucket or pot. Or you can let them take pots and pans out of a low kitchen cupboard and put them back in it.

## ACTIVITIES FOR TODDLERS

Older babies, of about fifteen months to two-and-a-half years of age, are learning to balance, walk, and talk. They are always on the go, and life is a constant adventure—for both you and the toddler. The toddler is developing very fast physically and enjoys playing in ways that promote his new abilities.

### Playthings.

- Balloons and soft balls are fun to chase after and try to catch.
- Toddlers love push-and-pull toys, small wagons, and pushcarts. They will climb in and out of a stroller and "help push."
- Large cardboard crates are also great to climb in and out of; large cardboard tubes make tunnels to crawl through.
- There are some small trikes and riding toys for toddlers. Watch out for models that tip too easily, as this can be a frustrating experience for the child.
- Nesting eggs or toys can be taken apart and put together.
- Plastic jars with tops can be screwed and unscrewed. Or try putting beads in them to shake and make noise.

- Empty cans with no sharp edges can be stacked, rolled, or used for putting things in and out of.
- Wooden beads are fun to string and wear for necklaces or just pull around on the floor.
- Old magazines are good to look at and name things. How about making a scrapbook of animals and their babies for a toddler?
- Toddlers love soft cuddly animals to comfort and feel.
- Construction toys such as blocks can be made from soft lumber (see preschool toys). Toddlers also like to play with giant nesting blocks. These are the kind that stack and fit inside one another.
- Toy telephones encourage a toddler to talk. Mrs. B. says that she had a child who spoke in garbled language with the toy phone; when she asked the child's mother about this she learned that the mother spoke with the grandmother in Armenian on the phone. Don't be surprised if you hear yourself when the toddlers talk on the telephone!
- Dolls and play-house equipment, such as a set of dishes and some water, are good for beginning housekeepers.
- Playdough is a favorite. You can make it yourself with the recipe given on pages 26-27.
- Beanbags are made simply with dried beans or birdseed and cloth. Just buy a sack of birdseed and bake it for fifteen minutes at 250 degrees to sterilize it. Then cut out squares of Dacron or cotton (the older children can help with this) and sew.

## Games.

- Music and dancing
- Peek-a-boo behind cloth, your hands, books
- Playing with water (filling plastic cups, bottles, pots and pans)
- Playing with sand and spoons, shovels, and pots

- An instrument panel—look for one in thrift stores, or make your own—with switches to turn off and knobs to turn. (Old washing machines in junkyards can be stripped of their pushbutton panels!) This saves your TV.
- Cloth books such as *Pat the Bunny* that a toddler can look at and touch at the same time.

## ACTIVITIES FOR PRESCHOOLERS

Preschool children will use some of the toys and activities enjoyed by toddlers, but they will use them in different ways. They will need additional materials to stretch their thinking.

**Make believe and dramatic play.** Preschool children learn a lot through dramatic play and role playing. They act out roles of people (parents, doctors, firemen, nurses, anyone they happen to see), and by this have a better sense of what these people are.

Dramatic play serves another purpose as well: it allows the child to try out ways of behaving that are difficult in real life. It can be a way of working through emotions or otherwise unacceptable behaviors, as you see when a child spanks a doll. It can also be a way of examining feelings about experiences a child has had or wishes he did have. For instance, after children have seen a fireman or a fire, or heard adults talk about one or seen one on television, playing fireman may be a recurrent theme in their dramatic play. Or a shy, quiet child may build confidence for trying a new activity by playing "giant" or "strong man" (or woman), or the "leader." Such practice gained in "make believe" carries over to real life in important ways.

Here are some accessories to provide opportunities for dramatic play:

- Plastic dishes (or old dishes), pots and pans, a cardboard box turned upside-down for a table, an eggbeater, some towels—these are good things for a kitchen scene.

- A cash register, empty cans (save the labels), egg cartons, some paper money (you can make this), or exchange items such as pegs, golf tees, popsicle sticks—these can help start a store.
- Old letters and boxes with some old stamps, a "uniform," and an old leather bag, a mailbox— these make a good mail-delivery person.
- An old garden hose, hats, and cardboard boxes will make it fun to play fireman. How about visiting a nearby firehouse to really "spark" the play?
- Rubber play people or animals can be used with blocks or by themselves. Shoe boxes make great houses for these animals and people.
- Large appliance boxes from stoves and refrigerators are fine for setting up a make-believe house, with some clothes for dressing up: shoes, pocketbooks, wallets, scarves, hats of all sorts, jewelry and a half-slip for formal attire, glasses, gloves, aprons, white coats for bakers, nurses, and doctors, a mirror and a clothes rack for props. These will set off a lot of different types of play.

**Art experiences.** Preschoolers love to make things. They express themselves through drawing, crayoning, painting, sculpture, and putting objects together in many ways. Lots of encouragement about what's being made is helpful.

Sometimes a child's picture tells about a specific topic —the home, a trip, a new baby. Often a picture helps a child to "say" what he can't talk about. Sometimes it's "just a picture" and that's all.

Be honest in your appraisal of a young child's work; preschoolers know when you're "putting it on too thick." Don't overdo your praise.

*Collage* involves gluing things to something else; all you need is two or three different materials (to glue) in some containers on a work table, some glue, and some brushes (or Q-tips) and something to glue onto—paper, cardboard pieces, styrofoam, toilet paper rolls, cottage cheese lids, and so on.

Materials to glue with might include straws, cut-out shapes, buttons, egg shells, string or yarn, feathers, wood chips, sawdust, sand, macaroni, sequins, foam rubber, cork, beans, and seeds.

Here are two recipes for homemade paste:

1. No-cook paste (not a very sticky paste): Take a handful of flour, add a pinch of salt, and add water until the mixture is gooey.
2. Boiled paste: Put half a cup of flour in a pan. Add cold water until the mixture is as thick as cream. Simmer and stir five minutes on the stove. Store this paste in the refrigerator.

How about taking a walk outside to collect *natural* collage materials? These could be leaves, sticks, pine cones, seeds, feathers, sand, rock, sidewalk treasures, and other goodies. Some collages might be based on a specific idea such as shapes, paper strips, body parts, numbers, letters, or different smelling objects.

You can get materials for *painting* at art supply stores, hobby shops, or department stores. But these are often already mixed and usually expensive. There are alternatives that are cheap and good:

- Powdered tempera is inexpensive and goes a long way. It can be found in art supply stores and some department stores. Look at the directions on the container for the mixing procedure; you will need to add water and liquid laundry starch. Mix this to the right consistency for you.
- A thick paint can be made by mixing powdered tempera with a thick mixture of soap flakes and water. This is a good finger-painting concoction for toddlers. Mrs. F. uses this as a finger-paint in the bathtub with toddlers and preschoolers. After the painting is finished, you wash everything (kids, equipment, and the tub), and then have a bath.

• Starch paint can also be made as follows: Combine one cup liquid laundry starch, six cups water, one-half cup soap flakes, and tempera or food coloring. Dissolve the soap in water until there are no lumps; mix well with the starch; color with tempera or food coloring.

*Brushes* with thick long handles for little hands to grasp are easiest for young children. "Kindergarten brushes" are one inch wide and have hardwood handles. They last quite a while. Clean your brushes in cold water and soap and store them in a can or wrapped in newspaper. Most art supply stores or stores with children's toys will have these brushes.

Other implements to paint with include fingers for finger painting, sponges that can be cut in different sizes and shapes for sponge painting, eye droppers for drip painting, and straws for blow painting.

Improvise *paint containers* by using tin cups, old muffin tins, egg boxes, cottage cheese or yogurt containers, orange juice cans, and so on.

*Paint surfaces* might include paper (newsprint is cheap), burlap, shiny shelf paper, wax paper, cardboard, or styrofoam. Observe how the paint is absorbed by the different textures. An easel can be made by fastening a large sheet of plywood with hinges to a wall so that it swings down.

Old shirts make good "cover-ups" for young artists. Some paints are hard to wash off, and some colors, such as red, are usually hard to get out of clothes. Make sure the children don't have on their Sunday best with these paints.

There are a variety of drawing implements to use in addition to paints. These include magic markers or non-toxic watercolor pens, chalk, and thick pencils and crayons. Experiment with these on different textures of paper. Children are fascinated by the different results when crayons or magic markers are used first on construction paper and then on shelf paper. On construction paper the color is softer and more absorbed by the paper. On shiny shelf paper, the color is more vivid and bold.

*Soap crayons* are good for play in the bath, as they can be easily washed off walls and bodies. (Older children might like to use these for make-up, too.) To make soap crayons mix 1/8 cup water with a little less than one cup of Ivory soap flakes. Stir until the soap and water have become a smooth, thick paste, and then add a good deal of food coloring. Press the mixture firmly into a mold, such as plastic ice-cube trays or popsicle molds. Let dry in a warm place for one or two days, until the paste is hard, and then remove from the tray.

Mrs. B. made an art gallery with her kids, hanging special paintings on the walls and on the refrigerator. She helped the four- and five-year-olds write their names on their paintings, and the older children wrote the toddlers' names on their creations. Then the eight-year-old helped frame the works with construction paper and put paper hooks on the backs so that they could be hung. Parents were invited in to look at the paintings, and the children also went with Mrs. B. to an art museum to see how other galleries look.

Another provider helps the children make notebooks of their creations. They back paintings with construction paper or newspaper and then present them to parents on Mother's Day or birthdays.

How about a neighborhood art show with the older children? With your help they could organize to show their own art work in a place where the whole neighborhood could view it.

**Modeling materials.** Toddlers, preschoolers, and older school-age children will play with playdough endlessly. You can make it yourself with:

| | |
|---|---|
| 2½ cups flour | ½ cup water |
| 1 cup salt | Food coloring |
| 2 tbsp. vegetable oil | |

Mix all together and knead for a few minutes until thick, like cookie dough. You may add the coloring either by mixing a few drops of color into the water beforehand, or by adding a few drops of color to the dough mixture and kneading it in, which results in a swirly, rainbow effect.

Dough keeps well in a plastic bag.

The children can make shapes and then eat them with this recipe for peanut butter playdough. Simply mix peanut butter, powdered milk, and honey until they are of a consistency good for modeling.

Baker's clay can be made in large batches. The proportions are 4 parts flour, 1 part salt, and 1½ parts water. Mix well, until the dough is stiff. Then shape things with it. This dough isn't very good to eat, but you can let it dry or bake it in a very slow oven for an hour or so and then paint it, for some interesting effects.

Some good tools for modeling dough are forks, rolling pins, pencils, shells, leaves, twigs, toothpicks, and blunt knives.

Snow is a delightful free (and sometimes plentiful) material, and exploring snow in the comfort of the house is a cozy winter activity. A good way to do it is to offer a large tub or dishpan of clean snow on a waterproof surface such as an old plastic tablecloth or shower curtain spread on the floor. The children can help collect the snow. Supply them with a variety of containers and kitchen utensils. Foil pans from frozen pot pies are good to use as cookie cutters, jello molds, measuring cups, and spoons. Let the kids pack the dishes with "cakes and pies." Expect that they will want to taste each other's bakery delights. If you want, you can add food coloring and brushes to the activity so that the children can decorate their creations. Or as a special treat, cake decorations can be added. Older children may guess the way to "keep" their pies—that is, put them back in the big refrigerator outdoors.

Mrs. A. says her children wear their mittens while modeling snow! And Mrs. S. lets her children make colored snow waterfalls outside. Add food coloring to snow and water in the driveway or gutter, near a drain, or on a hill, and watch it flow.

**Woodworking.** Working with wood is a good way to let off steam. It also helps children develop their eye-hand coordination and learn to solve building problems. Supply the children with the following tools and materials:

- Lightweight hammers (12–18 oz.)
- Sandpaper
- Screwdrivers—short stubby ones work the best
- Screws—large ones with wide heads are good
- C-clamps or a vise for holding pieces of wood
- Hand saws—ones with 14 to 18 teeth per inch work best
- Nails—2d, 3d, or 4d common nails or 1-inch galvanized roofing nails are easiest to hit with a hammer
- Hand drills—the "egg beater" type are fun to use
- Planes—these are available in small sizes, but they have sharp edges and take some supervision
- Rulers
- Pencils—flat carpenter pencils are the real thing to use
- Wood—two-by-four lumber scraps are best and can be found in scrap piles at building sites or lumber yards; soft wood such as pine is easiest for young children to work with
- Pieces of corrugated cardboard or styrofoam, which make good substitutes for wood to saw and hammer
- Other odd materials such as wooden spools and wires.

You can make a workbench for the kids, but a two-foot-square board on the floor, covered with carpet scraps to muffle sounds, works fine. This can be used indoors and out. Mrs. F. got some free painter's hats and carpenter's aprons at her local hardware store for her young carpenters.

**Construction toys.** There are many toys that children can build things with, mostly involving putting together little pieces in different and creative ways. This is very good for developing small muscles, particularly those in the fingers. Some children's favorites include:

- Beads with large holes and yarn for stringing them together.
- Tinkertoys, Lego, Bristle Blocks, design cubes, and table building blocks.
- Lacing boards with laces.
- Puzzles. (Twelve to thirty pieces are best for preschoolers. When selecting puzzles remember that the more pieces to fit together, the harder the puzzle is.)
- Pegboards and pegs.
- Geoboards and elastics.

Because of the tremendous variety of construction toys available, it is a good idea to look through catalogues before you buy any materials. Some school suppliers have free catalogues with extensive lists of preschool materials and pictures and descriptions of each item. Some of the established school suppliers are:

ABC School Supply
427 Armour Circle N.E.
Atlanta, Georgia 30325

Beckley-Cardy Company
1900 N. Narragansett Avenue
Chicago, Illinois 60639

Constructive Playthings
1040 East 85th Street
Kansas City, Missouri 64131

J. L. Hammett Company
Braintree, Massachusetts 02184

The Montgomery Schoolhouse, Inc.
Montgomery, Vermont 05470

Preschoolers really enjoy block play, and without much effort or expense you can make a set of blocks. Remind the children that blocks are to take care of, not to hammer on.

- *Pine Blocks.* Pine is good material for wooden blocks; it is relatively inexpensive and easy to use, does not splinter, and sands easily. Just cut up some two-by-fours (long boards that are four inches wide and two inches thick) into pieces of varying size. This is a joint project for you and the children, with you cutting the blocks and the children helping to sand them smooth.
- *Box Blocks.* Boxes with lids (gift boxes, stocking boxes, food packages, etc.) can be taped shut to make giant building blocks. Egg cartons and milk containers also make good blocks. You and the children can decorate these with drawings.
- *Tin Cans.* Coffee cans or other cans with plastic lids also make good blocks; glue the tops on.

Tin cans or juice cans also make good stilts. Older children can help you and the younger ones make these. Punch holes in the closed ends of large juice cans. Put a piece of rope about five feet long through these holes and tie the ends together. Make two of these, one for each foot. Stand on the cans, hold onto the rope—and walk slowly at first, as they wobble!

**Games.** Playing games and finding out about rules is an important pastime for young children.

Lotto is good for matching objects; and you can make your own lotto games by cutting out pictures to match with each other, or by drawing numbers and letters on a large sheet and matching them with cards of numbers and letters. Mrs. S. makes lotto games with cereal boxes. Taking two cereal boxes of the same kind, she cuts up one and leaves the other whole. The children must take turns placing the cut pieces together, and the object is to complete a card just like the whole one.

Card games like "Go Fish," "Animals," "Birds," and "Fish" are always popular.

There are some games that you play in your head without the need of any materials. School-age children will like these games and may want to make up their own versions. Two examples are the "Opposite Game," in which you think of something and say it and the child must think of the opposite (hot-cold, sunny-?); and the "Riddle Game," in which you think of something and give a hint, and the players must guess it ("I'm thinking of something that is blue and has wings . . . ?).

Here are some other games you can make easily:

- "Guess What the Smell Is." Assemble a collection of any of the following and have the children cover their eyes and guess what it is by smelling (cinnamon, vanilla, cloves, tobacco, tea, perfume, pepper, vinegar, talcum, mint, peels of lemon and orange, onions, garlic, balsam, and so on).

- "What Does It Feel Like?" Put a number of different objects in a bag and try to guess what they are by feeling, before pulling them out. Vary the textures (metal, plastic, wood, soft and hard, and the like).

- "What Floats, What Sinks?" Experiment with a variety of objects in water. Try to guess whether the object will float or sink before placing it in the water (soap, empty milk cartons, utensils, an egg, pieces of egg cartons, pine cones, straws, stones, sponges). Ask: What is heavy? Light? Will this heavy thing sink? Or Float?

- "Toss." Try tossing large colored buttons, spools, crumpled newspaper, and so on, into a box. The skill of tossing becomes a game—if the child can get them all in, get in more than you, count what he or she gets in, etc.

- "Stick and Hat." Put a hat on the top of a broomstick or a long tube. Children can try to knock it off by throwing sponges or other light objects. The height of the stick can be changed to make it harder.

- "Bowling Alley." Set up a number of cartons in a hallway or a driveway and have the children try to knock them over by rolling small or large cans or softballs.

**Musical instruments you can make.** You and the children can make some basic rhythm instruments to accompany yourselves, give yourselves or the neighbors a concert, or have a parade.

- *Drums.* Oatmeal boxes make good drums. Cover them tightly with some glue or tape, decorate them, and play.
- *Cymbals.* Two pot covers or two tin pie plates make fine cymbals when you bang them together.
- *Bells.* Bells can be strung on a piece of yarn or attached to a wrist or ankle for shaking.
- *Guitars.* You can make a guitar with some string and a half-gallon milk carton or a piece of wood or cardboard. Cut five slits in the top of the milk carton (or on the top and bottom of the wood or cardboard). Cut a square hole about two inches by two inches on one side of the carton; then wind the string around the carton, through a slit and over the hole. Make about five strings. Strum the guitar by moving fingers along strings over the hole.
- *Noisemakers.* Fill plastic containers with rattling materials such as macaroni, rice, or small buttons— and put the lids on tight!

## HOW ABOUT THE AFTER-SCHOOL CHILD?

The older child coming from a day at school has individual needs too. Often it is helpful to provide some sort of transition between school and home. A hug and a smile, a few moments for talking about the day, eases him into the new situation. And don't forget a snack, as he will be hungry.

A lot of after-school children come in saying, "What's there to do?" With a little planning, there are plenty of answers. Sometimes letting a child choose his own activities helps to balance out a day in school where his activities are mostly chosen for him.

Here are some long-term continuing projects that can be picked up by the child after school:

- Model cars, boats, and airplanes to put together.
- Scraps of wood, hammers, and nails for woodworking (with some paint to finish the creations with).
- Paints, crayons, chalk, paper.
- Clay and modeling materials.
- Cardboard or burlap scraps for drawing or painting on.
- Construction paper to frame paintings or to make things from.
- A garden to work in.
- A weather chart to note temperatures and weather daily.
- A wind barometer.
- Table games (checkers, jigsaw puzzles, cards).
- A car wash in the warm weather (your car, the neighbor's).
- A play to put on for the younger ones (make the costumes and sets).
- Collections (butterflies, rocks, shells, you name it).
- Community groups or classes at the local Y.M.C.A., Y.W.C.A., or other local civic or religious organizations.
- Storytelling at the local library.
- If space permits, how about a fort outside?

Some activities might call on the older child to be responsible—such as doing a special task with the younger children, not a demanding one, but one he feels good about (playing catch, playing traffic man).

Lots of exercise is in order after a day of sitting at desks. Be prepared.

## READING BOOKS WITH CHILDREN

Reading is:

—a time to sit on laps and be cuddled;

—a chance to learn new words and new ideas;

—a time to tell about what you've seen or done (a book about a storm on a stormy day gives everyone a lot to talk about and relate to);

—a way to help sort out feelings (*A Friend Is Someone Who Likes You* is a good book for this);

—a good way to stir your imagination and transport you to the make-believe;

—a chance to participate, to help turn pages, make sounds of animals, trucks, and people, fill in words you already know, act out the story.

Don't worry about your reading ability. The children won't care. The story you like will come through to them the best.

Mrs. R. made a book with her children:

> Tommy had an elephant friend that he talked a lot about. I knew that kids like to have a friend who is make-believe to talk things over with, so I wasn't too upset. I was amused when Tommy said his elephant friend wanted to visit some zoo elephants. We all took a trip to the zoo where children could feed peanuts to the two elephants that lived there. When we returned home, Tommy and the other kids drew pictures of the zoo and of our trip in the bus. I wrote down under the pictures what the children said about them and then added a few sentences of my own to piece things together. We put the pages in a spiral notebook and it's one of our favorite stories to read.

You can also make books by cutting out pictures in magazines and making up a story about them. Older children like to write and illustrate comic books. You might look in thrift stores for old copies that could be cut up and used for ideas.

Check at your library for editions of books in other languages, such as Spanish, that might be more meaningful to you or to the children. Libraries also have children's books that are specifically about children of different ethnic, racial, or religious backgrounds.

Some people concerned about sex stereotyping in children's books have written about and suggested books that don't perpetuate the traditional male and female images. For a free catalogue of nonsexist children's books, send a self-addressed envelope with your request to: Lollipop Power, Inc., Box 1171, Chapel Hill, North Carolina 27514.

When a child says, "Read it again," after you read a book once, it is a sure sign that the book is appropriate. In the last chapter of this book I have included a list of favorite books for children of different ages.

## MUSIC AND MOVEMENT

Singing and dancing are activities that come naturally to children. They love to make up songs, to learn new songs and sing old ones, and to dance about, experiencing the ways their bodies move. Don't worry about whether you can carry a tune—the children won't be judging you.

It is worth investing in a few songbooks and records to share with the children. In the last chapter of this book I have included a list of several that are favorites in many homes, and some places to order them. Or how about making your own songbook in a looseleaf binder—putting in your old favorites and some originals, too?

Records don't have to be especially for children in order that they enjoy the music. Folk songs, classical music, even popular rock, are all fun for the children to dance to. A good variety helps children to learn to move in different ways and to discriminate between various sounds and rhythms.

## IDEA BOOKS FOR YOU

The Association for Childhood Education International (A.C.E.I.) puts out some helpful books for parents and caretakers. *Play, Children's Business* is a guide to selection of toys and games for infants to twelve-year-olds. *Bits and Pieces: Imaginative Uses for Children's Learning* is another useful book. Write: A.C.E.I., 3615 Wisconsin Avenue, N.W., Washington, D.C.

*The Toy Book* by Steven Caney (Workman Publishing) is a paperback on how to make simple toys, musical instruments, and science toys.

Vicki Cobb has written two helpful books, *Arts and Crafts You Can Eat* and *Science Experiments You Can Eat,* both published in paperback by Lippincott.

The Edmund Scientific Company (EDSCORP Building, Barrington, New Jersey 08007) has a free catalogue of low-cost equipment for hobbyists and aspiring scientists, which includes everything from weather balloons to your own laser-beam machines.

Parents As Resources, or PAR (464 Central Avenue, Northfield, Illinois 60603), is a group of parents who have compiled at least two beautiful books of things to do with "saved" household materials. Their books are: *Recipes for Fun (Recetas Para Divertirse* in Spanish), *More Recipes for Fun,* and *Holiday Recipes for Fun.*

The Perry Nursery School (1541 Washtenaw Avenue, Ann Arbor, Michigan 48104) has published *The Scrap Book,* a collection of activities and recipes for preschool children.

*How Children Learn,* by E. Pitcher, M. Lasher, S. Feinburg, and N. Hammon, and published by Charles E. Merrill, is a meaty presentation of ways in which children learn and the materials that promote learning.

Project Headstart (Office of Child Development, Department of Health, Education, and Welfare, Washington, D.C.) puts out *Beautiful Junk,* a pamphlet with suggestions for outdoor play. It is available from the National Association for Nursery Education, 155 East Ohio Street, Chicago, Illinois.

## 4. THE COMMUNITY AND YOU

THE COMMUNITY in which we live has so many resources for young children and adults. It offers places to go, people to help, and materials to scrounge.

### PLACES TO GO WITH CHILDREN

Young children love to get out and go places. Errands that might seem ordinary and routine to you are adventures for them. Even going to pick up some milk down the street or some vegetables at the grocery store is fun. Take time to explain what goes on in each place.

*Airports:* There are many small airports in every state, and every major city has a large airport. Children love to watch planes land and try to guess where they are coming from. Mrs. G. took her children to a municipal airport near her home. "We got to see the small planes take off and land, and even sat inside one with the pilot, looking at the instrument panel."

*Arboretums:* These are places where you can look at exotic plants and flowers in botanical gardens. How about a visit during the different seasons to compare the differences in the plants? This is a good place to walk off some of the pent-up winter energy!

*Aquariums:* Many large cities have aquatic museums or aquariums. Here the children can see exotic fishes and other kinds of sea life. Find out if you can get a special group admission rate.

*Audubon Society:* Mrs. P. took her day care children to the local Audubon Society. "We explored nature with Audubon people who helped us discover all about living things and even rock formations. Did you know a drumlin is a form of hill left by glaciers? Well, we learned that. And then we had a picnic among all of the birds, raccoons, and even an owl or two, which hooted while we ate."

*Bakeries:* The bakery business is fascinating to watch and wonderful to smell! Call ahead and see if the bakery is willing to have you come and if they can show you around. (Dunkin' Donuts is usually friendly, and even gives free samples.) Mrs. D. takes her children to visit a fresh bagel shop: they get a tour of the bakery and can ask lots of questions about what makes different kinds of bagels—egg, onion, pumpernickel, sesame, and so on. Did you know that bagels are not made like doughnuts (which are made by cutting a hole), but instead are formed by twisting one piece of dough in a circle? Best of all is taking home a bag of warm bagels!

*Construction Sites:* Children can see huge machinery and workers in work clothing and hard hats. This will spark the preschool children's dramatic play when they return to your home. Most towns and cities always have ongoing construction projects to watch.

*Florist or Greenhouse:* This is a good place to learn about different kinds of plants. Stepping into a warm greenhouse with its moist air gives you and the children a real understanding of what atmosphere plants need to grow. Some florists, if you call ahead and ask, will give you a tour.

*Fire Houses:* This is a very exciting trip for children. They can look at the shiny fire engines and fire-fighting equipment, and talk with the firemen.

*Museums:* Young children love to go to museums, especially ones specializing in autos, trains, dolls, science, and other cultures, such as Eskimos or Indians. Some museums have special exhibits for children, and special children's rates on certain days.

*Parks:* Most states are full of beautiful parks and historical places to explore. These are usually free, and some parks are particularly well thought out for young children, with special climbing equipment and swings. Contact the regional department of parks and recreation (look under Government, Parks and Recreation in the yellow pages of the telephone book) for information about places near you.

*Picnics:* How about a picnic at a beach, pond, lake, stream, or bog? Young children love to explore the animal and plant life in these places. It's a chance to roll up your pants and wade in water and wriggle your toes in the sand. Or, you can fish or catch worms, or sail paper boats you made yourself!

*Police Stations:* Policemen often are very willing to show children their badges, uniforms, radios, fingerprinting devices, and to give a tour of the station.

*Post Offices:* Have you ever tried writing a letter to yourself and mailing it at the post office? Some post offices will agree to show you around in the back where they sort the mail. Children can buy stamps to put on their letters and then mail them to themselves. They can learn all about the mailing process and better understand the how and why of letters appearing on their doorsteps.

*Zoos:* There are zoos and wild animal farms in many different areas. Here children have an opportunity to see live animals that they have heard so much about in books. Mrs. D. takes her day care children to the children's zoo at least once every year. Getting there takes a 45-minute drive, "but it's worth it." She teams up with another family day care provider and they load all of the kids, along with some books to help make the ride go faster, and sing all the way to the zoo. You can pet the animals, she says, and they are really tame. It's really a place "where kids and animals get together." Hours and admission fees differ for some zoos in the winter and in summer, so call ahead to find out what they are.

Keep your eyes open anytime you go someplace, as you might stumble on a possible trip. Talk with other family day care providers for ideas. There is also a fascinating book called the *Yellow Pages of Learning,* which describes in detail what might be learned from just about anyone in your community. (What can you learn from a taxicab driver? an engineer? a mailman?) This book is available in many bookstores and is a handy guide for exploring the community with children. Written by the Group for Environmental Education (GEE), it was published by the M.I.T. Press in 1972. Many large cities have resource books of places to take children. Check your bookstore or library.

## SCROUNGING

Many useful play and learning materials can be obtained at no charge from organizations and stores right in your community. Here are some suggestions:

*Airlines:* Plastic cups.

*Architectural firms:* Blueprint and drafting paper, color samples, wood scraps.

*Billboard companies:* Brilliant pieces of billboard to use as posters, wall coverings, giant puzzles.

*Bottling firms:* Bottle caps, large cardboard tubes.

*Carpet stores:* Samples of discontinued rug patterns, soft foam.

*Cleaners and tailors:* Buttons, hangers, scrap materials.

*Clothing manufacturers:* Cloth scraps for sewing.

*Container companies:* Large cardboard sheets.

*Contractors and building supply companies:* Lumber, pipes, wire, linoleum, tiles, molding wood, wood curls, sawdust. (You can arrange to go to a construction site when they are finishing a job and they will let you collect scrap building materials.)

*Department stores:* Fabric swatches (drapery and upholstery supplies), rug swatches, corrugated packing cardboard, sample food cans and boxes, large packing boxes.

*Electric power companies:* Telephone poles, wooden cross arms, steel ground rods, wire, large spools that make good tables, and packing materials. (Call the company's public relations department.)

*Electronics firms:* Styrofoam packing, printed circuit boards, discarded components, colored wires.

*Engineering firms:* Blueprint paper for drawing and painting, computer cards.

*Fabric stores:* Inner cardboard forms make good plaques for artwork; ribbon scraps, cloth pieces.

*Furniture factories:* Turned wood scraps.

*Garment factories, button manufacturers:* Yarn, buttons, scraps, decorative tape, remnants.

*Gas stations:* Tires for swings, tractor tires for sandboxes, bottle caps for collages, old steering wheels that can be fastened to a crate to make a good "car."

*Grocery stores:* Boxes of all sizes for all purposes, packing materials, large cardboard and pictures for display, styrofoam fruit packing trays.

*Hardware stores:* Sample hardware books, sample tile charts.

*Ice cream stores:* Empty three-gallon cardboard containers which make good cubbies and space helmets.

*Junkyards:* A gold mine of possibilities! Wheels of all shapes and sizes, all kinds of gears and moving parts from clocks, radios, fans, irons, cars, toasters, and so on. Handles for doors, knobs, broomsticks, hinges, and fittings. You name it.

*Large food and candy manufacturers:* Sample cans and boxes.

*Moving companies:* Large wooden crates to turn into playhouses.

*Paint shops:* Color cards to learn colors, old paint brushes for water painting, cardboard paint buckets, hats.

*Paper companies:* Different kinds of paper are often available free, in the form of samples, or cut and/or damaged sheets. Paper is usually delivered to the companies in large tubes that make good chairs, tables, and storage units.

*Plastics companies:* Trimmings, scrap plexiglass and plastic.

*Plumbers and plumbing supply companies:* Wires, pipes, tile and linoleum scraps.

*Pocketbook, belt, and shoe manufacturers:* Scrap pieces of leather, laces, etc.

*Rug companies:* Sample swatches and pieces from rugs. You can make a patchwork rug by gluing various swatches together with wallpaper glue on a piece of canvas.

*Shoe stores:* Stacking boxes with shoe boxes or stocking boxes.

*Telephone company:* Large empty reels, spools, colored wires. They will lend you some telephones and will rent film strips, movie projectors, etc. (Call the public relations department.)

*Tile stores:* Unused or unmatched pieces of tile, good for sorting, counting, matching, and creating.

*Wallpaper stores:* Books of discontinued wallpaper patterns, used textured sheets for painting.

Where can you put all of these materials? Empty three-gallon ice-cream containers or large boxes can be stacked for storage of these scrounged items. Mrs. D. puts a picture of the item on each box so that children can recognize where things are. She also makes storage units of large paper tubes from paper companies to help solve the perpetual toy storage problem. In these tubes she puts toys, clothes, collage materials, and such. She cuts the tubes to a length of about 18 inches and then bolts them together in a triangle formation for the storage unit.

Collecting materials to be discarded and using them in the home provides an excellent model of behavior for young children. They watch you and learn where things come from and, more important, some alternatives to where they might go—besides the dump.

What to do with all of this? Young children are so creative that the materials are limited only by the child's imagination, and yours. Experimentation with and combining of varied materials provide endless activities and projects.

## PEOPLE IN THE COMMUNITY

Besides professional persons you might call when you have a specific need (doctors, lawyers, psychologists, social workers, accountants), there are people who can be very helpful to you as a day care provider in your home.

**Extra hands.** Do you know another person who provides family day care in your community and could work with you as a *back-up provider?* Another provider can help with sharing the care when you are sick or on vacation, when you have a doctor's appointment, or when you want to take the older children on a trip and leave the younger ones behind. Providers have found back-up persons by asking around the neighborhood, asking the local licensing worker if she knows of anyone nearby, putting up notices in the supermarket and laundromat, and keeping their eyes open for someone taking care of children.

   *Students* in local high schools and colleges are often interested in working with young children in homes. Some high schools (both vocational and regular) have programs in family planning and child development (under the home economics or health departments). Many community colleges have departments specializing in child development or early childhood education. Get in touch with the people in these places. Students might be available to help you in your home either on a regular basis or once in a while. These young people can really learn a lot from you while working in your home.

   One provider who called a high school was asked to come in (with a baby or two) and talk about child development in a class. Afterwards, some students came to her home to see her in action.

   *Elderly citizens* are often willing to help out as "foster grandparents" in working with children. Do you know an elderly person who might like to come in and do something (read stories, work with the older children) one afternoon a week? Get in touch with a senior citizens' group. A good place to leave word is at public libraries and local elementary schools, which often have events scheduled for elderly groups and provide meeting places for them.

   *Girl Scouts, Boy Scouts, Campfire Girls, and Boys' Clubs* are eager to help with young children. They can earn badges and learn a lot by doing so, but they do need some supervision. Contact the local troops.

   *Volunteer organizations* (listed under "Volunteer" in the yellow pages) often can suggest persons to help you in your home.

**Someone to talk with.** There is no question about it—it is very easy to feel isolated in your own home with young children. The idea of going out, of putting on four snowsuits, boots, hats, scarves, and mittens for a winter's walk, sometimes seems to be a tremendous undertaking. Or the thought that you can only go as far as those little legs will comfortably go, unless you are to carry everyone home, is a bit overwhelming at times.

Taking care of children is really a fulfilling experience. There are often times, however, when you would like to have some adults to talk with. As one family day care provider phrased it, "I need some emotional support." Whether it is just for seeing and talking with someone over three feet tall, or to talk about issues involving the children (napping, toileting, eating), or just to "pass the time," it makes sense.

As Mrs. F. says:

> ... some friends don't come over to have a cup of coffee because I can't give them all of my attention. I love having the kids, but I sure do love to have a neighborly chat with friends, too; and I do need it.

Some family day care providers have suggested the buddy system as a help. Very often someone else who is experiencing, or has experienced, the same thing, is helpful to talk with. Mrs. A. and Mrs. P. have arranged a buddy system; each call the other when she needs to talk or get out. Mrs. P. explains:

> It all started when one day I was walking in the park with my children. I was a little worried about the baby (13 months) who fussed and cried whenever we went out. Mrs. A. happened along with her brood and saw us. She knew that I was a provider right off and we started talking. She had a child who did the same thing my baby does on walks. Mrs. A. said she thought it was because the baby was afraid of strange persons and places. She tried to bring along a familiar toy in the stroller for the baby. Every time she stops for a moment, she holds the baby with him facing her so that he is reassured that she hasn't left. I thanked her for the advice and we exchanged phone numbers. Now we call each other all the time to talk about everything from the baby's first tooth to our new diets!

Another person to talk with might be someone interested in child development. These people are usually very willing to talk about anything concerning young children and their care, parents, and day care providers.

They have a lot of useful know-how about young children. Here are some possible contacts:

- A local college with an early childhood program; they may have a teacher or professor with whom you can talk, or they may be able to suggest someone.
- A family day care system in your area; these often have people called "coordinators" for family day care homes who can provide useful information and an ear for listening.
- A local women's group might help out. These are often found connected with the Y.W.C.A.

## EDUCATIONAL RESOURCES AROUND YOU

There are educational resources out there for you, as well as for the children. Many community colleges, state colleges and universities, adult education programs, high schools, organizations, and state departments offer continuing education programs for interested adults.

- Health, accident, and safety training is usually available through the local Red Cross or the city or regional health department. The health departments offer courses and/or information on lead paint testing and procedures.
- Advice on food, nutrition, and meal planning may be obtained from the local health department or the extension service of the U.S. Department of Agriculture, the Dairy Council of America, or a nearby college or high school. (See Chapter 5, *Nutrition.*)
- Courses for persons who care for young children are offered by local community colleges, high school adult education programs, vocational programs, and universities. Other groups who offer workshops include libraries and the local affiliate chapters of the National Association for the Education of Young Children (N.A.E.Y.C.).
- A large variety of courses (everything from belly dancing to self-defense) is offered by the Y.M.C.A., Y.W.C.A., Jewish centers, black cultural centers, Boys' and

Girls' Clubs, adult learning centers, and so on. The fees are low.

The bureau of adult services of your state's department of education has information on courses being held for adults throughout the state. Ask them for current course listings, and for details on their high-school credit correspondence courses and noncredit courses to meet a variety of needs and interests. For information on obtaining a high-school diploma equivalency, write to the Adult Education Association of the U.S.A., 1225 19th Street N.W., Washington, D.C. 20036.

# 5. NUTRITION

YOUNG CHILDREN need food that helps them grow and keep well. Knowing about the individual child and his needs helps you make a good fit between the child and his food.

Try to find out beforehand, if possible, about known *food allergies* of the children. Some common foods that cause allergic reactions are eggs, chocolate, corn, cane sugar, citrus, milk, and wheat. Some information on symptoms of allergies would enable you to spot them and make some substitutions.

A young child is an individual. Different children have different appetites; some are big eaters, some are small eaters. All children seem to go through eating jags—when they will want to eat the same food over and over again—and then they may temporarily refuse to eat the very same food. If no great fuss is made about their preferences, this will pass.

## FOOD IS A PLEASANT EXPERIENCE

Bring the child and food together happily. Children don't eat as skillfully as adults do. But it is important to the child to "do it myself." Children will try to eat by themselves as soon as they can grasp the spoon. Learning to eat neatly depends on developing coordination and on trying it out for a while. A lot of praise and patience from you makes this a good experience. Also, use finger foods when possible.

Children won't get restless at the table if their food is served soon after they sit down.

New foods are more easily tasted if they are presented in small quantities. Serving small portions helps young children feel good about finishing. Now they will have a choice about coming back for more!

Being hungry is also a help—no snacks immediately before lunch. But nutritious eating is not necessarily three big meals a day. Young children seem to be constant snackers, and small stomachs need several small meals a day. Try to think of a total day's nutrition; if snacks before meals are a necessity, they should be part of the meal and not something extra.

Withholding snacks or desserts as a punishment, or using food as a reward, places exaggerated importance on particular foods. Also, dessert in some cases may be important for nutritional needs.

Young children really appreciate foods when they look good. It is worth the extra time to dress up salads with bright orange carrot shavings and to garnish dessert fruits, such as pears or applesauce, with a sprinkle of cinnamon. This provides children with a variety of colors and different textures to experience.

Eating together at meals is a good time for socialization, for talking with others, and for sharing. For children just as with adults, mealtime is a time to relax and to enjoy.

## MAKING MEALS MORE NUTRITIOUS

These days, it is no easy thing to provide nutritious meals. We all agree that it is important—good nutrition provides the necessary ingredients for health and growth.

For many children the meals and snacks at the day care home are their most nutritious food of the day. Working mothers often don't have the time and energy to prepare proper meals in the early morning or late evening hours. And sometimes they feel that meals take away from their time with the kids.

With food costs rapidly rising, family day care providers are met with a real challenge in providing nutritious meals and snacks! Many people strongly believe that good nutrition is as important to young children as an emotionally and intellectually nourishing environment. If "we are what we eat," it starts in infancy.

Many traditional snack products are not only expensive compared to whole foods, but are also nearly devoid of nutritional value. They may, in addition, contain food additives and coloring that are potentially harmful to children. Try to replace them with fresh or dried fruits, nuts, home-roasted pumpkin or sunflower seeds, fresh vegetables, peanut butter, and cheese, whenever possible.

Mrs. B. writes:

> I just quit having a traditional snack of crackers and juice
> . . . . The children asked me where the crackers were when I
> gave them cut-up carrots and celery or fruits and granola. I
> explained that crackers did not alone contain enough
> vitamins and nutrients for growth. We talked a lot about
> what the body needs to grow up big and strong. After a
> period of what I call "cracker withdrawal" the children
> began to ask for more nutritious snacks, and they now know
> *why* they wanted them!

How about trying honey as a sweetener? White sugar is known to be a nutritional zero. Mrs. H. began using honey when the price of sugar rose so fast. First she used it in baking; then she had it for table purposes. It makes a delicious snack on homemade bread! She and the children found out where honey comes from, and went to visit a man in town who keeps bees. They brought home some honeycomb and are all becoming bee experts. If there aren't any beekeepers near you, you might try just looking at a honeycomb and finding a good book about bees, or a nearby museum might have a bee exhibit.

More and more people are growing some of their own food. Consider the economics of a packet of seeds against the cost of the same produce in the market. Even started plants usually yield more than they cost. Is there really any comparison between homegrown vegetables and the commercial variety?

Encourage local produce growers, beef and poultry farmers, beekeepers, and the like by buying their products when available. It is exciting to learn where things come from, especially when they come from nearby and the children can see where. Mrs. A. says she asked her children where milk came from. One answered, "The store." So she took the children on a trip to a dairy, to see cows being milked. Her advice to others is to look up a dairy or farm near you—it's really worthwhile.

Some grocers will give you produce that they feel they cannot sell. Here is a good sorting activity for children to choose what can be saved and what can't, what is ripe and what is unripe, what is just right and what is rotten.

## YOU CAN MAKE YOUR OWN BABY FOOD

There's a lot of controversy about processed baby foods these days. People are spending extraordinary sums on those tiny jars, many of which contain unstated amounts of harmful sugar, salt, monosodium glutamate (M.S.G.), and modified starches.

It's cheap and easy to make your own baby food. Then you know what the food actually is that you are feeding to the baby. In addition, baby meals can be coordinated with the other children's (and yours) with no extra worry. Making pureed food takes only about two minutes of the time you spend preparing dinner for the others.

You will need to make a bit more effort at first, by getting a few supplies and reading a few books, perhaps. Here are some suggested supplies, recipes, and books.

A good food blender is a necessity. These can cost anywhere from $20 to $50, depending upon the type and where you get it. A Sears Roebuck blender is a good buy, according to Consumer Reports. Although this seems a large expense, think of it in terms of saving the money that mounts up when you buy those little jars. Blenders can be used for lots of other food preparations besides baby food, and most come with recipe books for incredible concoctions.

Some people find a table-model hand food grinder useful. This can cost from about $3 to $10. Grinders, which can be purchased in many department stores and supermarkets, can make about a cupful of food at one time. (The Happy Baby Food Grinder, made by Bowland-Jacobs Manufacturing Company, 8 Oakdale Road, Spring Valley, Illinois 61362, is a good one.)

Plastic ice-cube trays can simplify storage of infant foods; just pour in the food, freeze, and then pop out when it's time to use it.

A collection of storage jars and plastic containers (mini-blender jars, Tupperware's smallest size container, or odd-sized glass jars with lids—like your old empty baby-food jars) is necessary.

Plan to use some space in your refrigerator for storing baby food. It's easier to make double batches and then store one of them for another time, and you won't lose the nutrients or freshness in a day or two.

**Some basic foods for baby.** Around the age of four to six months (depending upon the baby, it may be before or after this time), babies become interested in some solid foods. Introduce new foods to a baby slowly; if there is a bad reaction to a particular new food, you will be able to pinpoint the cause. The easiest solids to start with are bananas, egg yolks, and yogurt.

*Banana:* Peel and mash one ripe banana. You can add a bit of milk, cereal, yogurt, or fruit to this for variety.

*Yogurt:* Plain unflavored yogurt is the most healthful; you can add fruit, cereal, or a bit of sweetening to this. Have you tried making your own yogurt? It's fun to do with older children, and many cookbooks give directions for doing it.

*Fruits:* Peel and cut any fruit (fresh is best, but you can drain the syrup from canned fruit if fresh is unavailable). Put the fruit in a blender with a bit of orange juice. Blend for a minute until it is of a sauce-like consistency that the baby can handle.

*Applesauce:* Beat one raw, peeled, and diced apple in the blender with one-fourth cup of apple juice. It can be chilled or eaten right away.

*Frozen fruits:* Peel any fruit—apple, banana, orange, strawberries—and put it in a freezer bag and freeze until solid. The fruit can be eaten frozen or partially thawed for a tasty treat for babies, children, or adults. Or, blend the partially thawed fruit in a blender for a delicious fruit sherbet.

*Cottage cheese fruit:* Blend quickly one-half cup cottage cheese, one-half cup fresh fruit (raw and peeled), and four to six tablespoons of juice. Spoon it. (Mrs. B. has a baby whose favorite food is cottage cheese and applesauce; he eats it like an adult eats an ice-cream sundae!)

*Meats:* After a few basic foods have been tried and tested, your baby might be ready to try out some meats. For infants, these are usually prepared as a kind of a stew.

### BEEF STEW

1 cup cubed or ground meat (beef or lamb)
¼ cup vegetables (carrots, green beans, peas, etc.)
¼ cup diced potato (sweet, white, or yam)
½ cup liquid (juice from cooking, water, or milk)

## CHICKEN AND RICE STEW

1 cup cubed chicken
¼ cup browned cooked rice (white or brown)
¼ cup vegetable
¼ cup chicken broth
¼ cup milk

For both of these recipes, steam all solids in a small pot with a little water, until just barely soft. Puree on high speed in the blender, with some water from the steamer. Pour into the freezer tray. When frozen, remove cubes as needed. Heat and serve (extra liquid may be needed). Each of the above recipes will fill a freezer tray; for storage over any length of time, cover with freezer wrap or tin foil.

*Vegetables:* These can be made much the same as meat. Steam cut-up raw vegetables for a little while until barely soft, and then puree in the blender.

*Finger foods for snacks and teething:* You really don't have to feed the baby yourself. It is okay for babies to use their fingers—their natural spoons and forks. When a baby is about a year old and has some teeth to chew with, he likes to snack on finger foods; these are great for older children and adults, too. Cut in small pieces and arrange on a platter fresh, raw cauliflower, carrots, celery, mushrooms, tomatoes, lettuce, sweet peppers, red and white cabbage, asparagus, shredded raw beets, apples, assorted melon balls, peas in the pod, or other fruits and vegetables in season.

Some infants are constant snackers. They will nibble on a piece of toast for hours until it is a mass of crumbs. They will never refuse an appetizing finger food. Day-old bagels make a great, non-messy teether and snack for babies. Or, for hot weather, try homemade popsicles.

*Popsicles:* This is an excellent sensory experience for toddlers, but babies need some manual control to manage them. Fill a popsicle tray with:

- equal parts apple, cranberry, and orange juice, or
- grape juice and yogurt in equal parts (delicious but messy), or
- orange juice, with extra vitamin C added if your child is sick, or
- milk with carob powder (1 teaspoon to 1 cup of milk) added and beaten in the blender (carob is a good and healthful chocolate substitute), or
- your own concoction.

Freeze for several hours until firm. Popsicles are great for a teething baby (coolness soothes the gums), or for a sick child who won't eat anything else.


## RECIPE IDEAS FOR OLDER CHILDREN

French toast, pancakes, or waffles can be prepared in advance, frozen, and the heated up in the toaster at snack time. Children love to do this; and it is a good science experiment when they see a frozen waffle change its form and become soft with heat. They can take a bite of the waffle frozen, and then warm, to compare.

*Individual pizzas:* Cover bread slices (English muffins or Syrian bread or bagels are good) with tomato sauce and a slice of cheese. Sprinkle on a pinch of oregano. Bake at 350 degrees until the cheese melts, and serve hot.

*Fruit kebobs:* No cooking for these, and they are fun to do with the children. You will need blunt-ended knives, plastic straws or toothpicks, one can of pineapple chunks, one peeled banana, and one pared apple cut in half-inch chunks. Place fruit on toothpicks or straws, alternating apple, pineapple, and banana. A special snack.

*Fruit milk shakes:* Mix one part fresh fruit, which the children can help cut up, with three parts milk and a little honey. Blend for a minute in a blender, if you have one, or beat with an eggbeater. Some variations on this: Use powdered milk—it's easy to mix, inexpensive, and very nutritious. Or, use a fruit juice base and powdered milk and blend for a scrumptious concoction.

There are many low-cost yet nutritious foods that children like. Old favorites include:

- Chicken, tunafish, and shell macaroni casserole
- Eggs (hard-boiled or in a salad)
- Bananas
- Pears
- Apples
- Strawberries
- Macaroni and cheese
- Cheese chunks
- Celery
- Raisins
- Granola
- Cocoa (hot cocoa can be made inexpensively with dry milk; a few drops of vanilla make it taste rich).

Children really like to make things from scratch. It gives them an opportunity to see how foods are really prepared and the natural ingredients that go into them. Here is a small collection of favorite recipes for children to help with.

## VEGETABLE SOUP

Arrange with the butcher at the local supermarket for a tour of the meat section and a discussion about meat bones on a day when you would like to make soup. Each child could bring a different vegetable or a spice from home. You will need:

- A large pot
- Beef bones
- 1 tablespoon vinegar
- Bay leaf
- 1 teaspoon thyme
- Parsley
- Cut-up carrots, celery, onions, potatoes, turnips, tomatoes, and any other vegetables

1. Put the bone(s) in the pot and cover with water.
2. Add spices and cook for a few hours.

3. Refrigerate and skim off the fat the next day.
4. Reheat, add salt if needed; add vegetables.
5. Cook until vegetables are tender.

Hint: Peel onions under water, or cut in quarters and slip off skins to avoid tears.

## CHICKEN SOUP

It seems that everyone has a different way to make this soup; this recipe is very basic, and the kids can help. You will need:

- A large pot
- A whole stewing chicken
- Bay leaf
- Parsley
- Thyme
- Salt
- Sage
- Carrots, celery, potatoes, onions, and turnips

1. Peel the vegetables, if necessary, and cut them up.
2. Put the chicken in the pot and add water or stock to cover.
3. Add the rest of the ingredients and simmer for 1 to 2 hours.
4. Refrigerate and skim off fat the next day.
5. Reheat and serve.

This is a very economical dish that hits the spot on a cold, stormy day.

## MEATBALLS WITH RICE

You will need:

- ¼ teaspoon salt
- ½ cup rice, uncooked
- 1 egg
- 1 tablespoon salad oil
- 1 small onion, chopped or grated

- 1 teaspoon thyme
- ½ teaspoon pepper
- 1 tablespoon parsley, chopped
- 2 cups tomato juice
- 1 pound ground beef or lamb

1. Mix all ingredients except tomato juice and shape into little balls; the children may want to shape their own.
2. Put meatballs in a pan that is large enough to hold them all in one layer.
3. Cook at 450 degrees for 15 minutes.
4. Take them out and pour tomato juice over them.
5. Cover pan with foil and put back in oven at 350 degrees for 1 hour.

## NO-BAKE OATMEAL COOKIES

- ½ cup honey
- ½ cup peanut butter
- 1 cup uncooked quick rolled oats
- 1 cup dry milk

1. Put the honey and peanut butter in a bowl and mix well.
2. Slowly add the dry milk and oatmeal; stir and mix well.
3. Make into small balls and refrigerate. Then eat.

Do you know an oatmeal cookie recipe that calls for cooking the cookies? Try both recipes and compare the cookies' taste, texture, and looks with the children.

## BANANA BREAD

- 2 bananas, well mashed
- 2 eggs, beaten until light
- 3 tablespoons honey
- 2 tablespoons soft margarine
- 2 cups flour
- ½ cup sugar

- ¼ teaspoon salt
- 2 teaspoons baking powder

1. Mix banana, honey, eggs, and margarine in a small bowl.
2. Sift other ingredients together and add to the banana mixture.
3. Mix well, pour into greased loaf pan, and bake at 350 degrees for 45 minutes.

How about making your own butter to spread on this bread?

## BUTTER

- 1 pint heavy cream
- Small glass jars, with tops (baby-food jars are good)

1. Put 1 tablespoon of cream in a jar and close it very tight.
2. Shake the jar for about 5 minutes (everyone gets sore arms, but don't give up).
3. All of a sudden, lumps of butter will start forming; pour off the liquid that remains, which is whey.
4. Mash all of the lumps of butter together, and add salt to taste, if desired.

Have you ever made your own peanut butter?

## PEANUT BUTTER

- 1 bag of peanuts (at least 1 pound)
- 1 to 2 tablespoons butter or peanut oil
- Salt
- Cloth bag
- Hammer

1. Have the children shell the peanuts (you might shell half of them beforehand, to avoid too long a task).
2. Put shelled nuts in cloth bag and let kids hammer them. The nuts should be broken into tiny pieces. This provides a good energy release.
3. Moisten with butter and sprinkle with salt.

Another way to make peanut butter is to shell the peanuts and then put them through a blender (or a meat grinder, if you have one) until they are ground up finely. Add enough oil to make the mixture the consistency of paste, and salt to taste.

## APPLESAUCE

- 3 to 5 pounds apples
- ½ cup sugar or honey

1. Peel the apples, if you like, and cut them up.
2. Put the pieces in a large saucepan and sweeten with sugar or honey.
3. Cook over medium heat until thick, stirring occasionally.
4. Strain the sauce (if you wish) through a food mill.

For some information about apples, you can write with the older children to the Washington State Apple Commission, P.O. Box 18, Wenatchee, Washington 98801. The commission provides a free instruction kit containing a recipe booklet and ideas for working with young children using the subject of apples.

## INSTANT PUDDINGS

These are fun to make with children, and even toddlers can help measure the milk, stir, and pour the mixture into cooking pans. Freezing pudding in ice-cube trays or dixie cups makes delicious popsicles.

## POPCORN

A good counting activity. Children can help measure oil and count the corn kernels. Comparing the popped corn and the kernels shows the different forms of corn.

## SNOW ICE CREAM — A WINTER SPECIALTY

- 1 egg, beaten
- 1 cup milk
- ½ cup sugar or maple syrup
- ½ teaspoon vanilla
- Dash of salt

1. Mix all ingredients in a large bowl.
2. Add about half a large bowl of clean snow.
3. Stir well, and dig in!

Maple syrup is a very expensive item these days, so you may want to substitute honey or just give the children a very little taste. But maple syrup and maple sugar used to be important sweeteners for people in years past; you might talk with the children about how it was used instead of our white sugar. If you are fortunate enough to live near some sugar maple trees, you might try your luck at tapping them with the children and making some syrup or sugar of your own.

## FRUIT SALAD

Have each of the children bring in one piece of fruit on a day when you would like to make a fruit salad. They can help peel or pare fruit and cut it up with blunt knives. Raisins, shredded coconut, and nuts are good on fruit salads. Children love to help toss the salad, with dressing. Tossing takes a lot of coordination of the upper arms of children. Watch them and be sure that your salad doesn't get sent into outer space!

## SNACKS

These are fun to prepare. Young children can cut up vegetables, spread fillings, and the like. Try dipping raw celery, cucumber, carrot sticks, or green pepper slices into cottage cheese mashed with a fork, or into yogurt. Or, stuff celery with cream cheese, peanut butter (a real favorite), or cottage cheese mashed with a fork.

Mrs. H. writes that she has peas in the pod as a summer snack. The children try to guess how many are in each pod. Then they open them up and count the peas. A sneak preview by holding the pod up to the light is okay, she says. This is a good counting game.

How about preparing a snack for Mom for when she comes to pick up her child? This might be helpful for a child having trouble with separation, or for a mom who needs to feel part of her child's day at another home.


## SOME SAMPLE MENUS

It frequently saves time and energy if you plan out a cycle of menus to use again and again. A three-week menu is usually sufficient and different cycles can be used during the various seasons, to take advantage of seasonal food buys. Also, you can show parents what the children are eating; some parents may have suggestions for recipes or special foods they prepare at home. Why not include special occasion menus for birthdays or holidays? Some day care providers set aside one day a week or month as a "favorite food day," when the children take turns having their favorite meals served.

Here's a sample three-week menu plan from a provider for toddlers, preschoolers, and older children:

## WEEK 1

|          | SNACK                              | LUNCH                                                               | SNACK                                                      |
|----------|------------------------------------|---------------------------------------------------------------------|-----------------------------------------------------------|
| **Mon.** | orange juice<br>peanut butter<br>  on celery | meat pot pie<br>raw carrot sticks<br>lime gelatin<br>bread & butter<br>milk | hot cocoa<br>cheese cubes                                 |
| **Tues.** | orange juice or<br>  apple slices | grilled cheese<br>  sandwich<br>celery sticks<br>fruit cocktail<br>bran muffin<br>milk | French toast<br>milk                                      |
| **Wed.** | apple juice<br>yogurt             | beef stew<br>cucumber salad<br>raisin & bread<br>  pudding<br>milk   | cream cheese on<br>  graham<br>  crackers<br>milk         |
| **Thurs.** | pineapple juice<br>  hash<br><br>carrot sticks | corned beef<br><br><br>hash<br>string beans<br>bread & butter<br>lemon pudding<br>milk | fruit milkshake                                           |
| **Fri.** | milk<br>raisins or nuts           | tuna salad on<br>  toast<br>cut corn<br>biscuit & butter<br>orange slices<br>milk | slice of hard-<br>  boiled egg, with<br>  dab of relish or<br>  peanut butter |

## WEEK 2

|  | SNACK | LUNCH | SNACK |
|---|---|---|---|
| **Mon.** | fruit juice punch (equal parts orange, cranberry & apple) cut-up vegetables | macaroni & cheese green peas fruit salad on lettuce chocolate pudding milk | yogurt with jam or fruit |
| **Tues.** | carob milk celery sticks | stewed chicken wings sliced beets noodles orange gelatin milk | apple slices spread with peanut butter |
| **Wed.** | pineapple juice peanuts in shell | fried bologna peach halves spinach bread & butter milk | celery stuffed with cream cheese cinnamon toast |
| **Thurs.** | apple juice carrot sticks | individual pizza potato salad chopped mixed vegetables strawberry gelatin milk | fruit kebobs |
| **Fri.** | orange juice raisins | spaghetti in sauce with meatballs tossed salad garlic bread pineapple slices milk | popcorn (the kids love to help) |

**WEEK 3**

| | SNACK | LUNCH | SNACK |
|---|---|---|---|
| **Mon.** | tomato juice<br>celery sticks | fish cakes<br>baked potatoes<br>sweet & sour<br>   green beans<br>applesauce<br>milk | waffles (made in<br>   advance, then<br>   heated in<br>   toaster) |
| **Tues.** | hot chocolate<br>apple slices<br>orange gelatin | hamburger on<br>   bun<br><br>baked beans<br>spinach<br>custard<br>milk | grated carrots in |
| **Wed.** | tomato juice<br>granola | black-eyed peas<br>   & ham<br>rice<br>kale<br>bread & butter<br>peach halves | fresh fruit salad |
| **Thurs.** | pineapple juice<br>carrot sticks | deviled eggs<br>tossed salad<br>stewed prunes<br>bread & butter<br>milk | milk<br>orange slices |
| **Fri.** | orange juice<br>toast & honey | chili con carne<br>cut corn<br>carrot sticks<br>crackers & butter<br>pineapple slices<br>milk | pancakes & jam<br>   (made in<br>   advance,<br>   frozen, and<br>   heated in<br>   toaster) |

## MENUS FOR INFANTS

|  | SNACK | LUNCH | SNACK |
|---|---|---|---|
| **Mon.** | orange juice<br>banana | pureed meat<br>  stew | milk or formula |
|  | banana | milk or formula |  |
|  | banana | stew<br>milk or formula | crusty bread,<br>  toasted |
| **Tues.** | milk or formula<br>applesauce | mashed egg<br>pureed celery<br>bananas<br>milk or formula | cottage cheese &<br>  fruit, mashed |
| **Wed.** | apple juice<br>yogurt | beef stew<br>pudding<br>milk or formula | graham cracker<br>milk or formula |
| **Thurs.** | pineapple juice<br>carrot sticks | pureed corned<br>  beef<br>pureed green<br>  beans<br>lemon pudding<br>milk or formula | fruit milkshake |
| **Fri.** | milk<br>orange sherbet<br>  (frozen orang-<br>  es pureed) | chicken stew<br>pureed carrots<br>apple slices<br>milk or formula | mashed egg<br>milk or formula |

## KIDS IN THE KITCHEN

Cooking is a rewarding experience for young children. It is not only great fun, but it is also a very educational activity. Children can explore the tastes, smells, colors, and textures of ingredients both in natural and combined forms. They are introduced to physical changes that take place when foods are cooked. Cooking allows children to become acquainted with new words to describe what is happening—stirring, boiling, bubbling, melting, sifting. They will use number concepts in measuring, and working with the tools of cooking helps develop manual dexterity. Often, cooking involves working in the forbidden realm of knives and fires, and children learn how to use these things wisely and safely.

Cooking with young children provides an opportunity for some activities involving the first steps in reading. How about making a cooking poster and illustrating the simple steps with pictures of the ingredients? Or, Mrs. C. made a cookbook with her children of "Our Favorite Things To Eat." The children cut out pictures of ingredients, and drew pictures of themselves cooking and tasting their "masterpieces."

Flops are also good experiences. Cookies that don't rise do happen. What matters in the cooking process is fun—not always the end result.

Helping out and seeing how foods are prepared often helps a finicky eater change into a good one. And in addition to everything else that makes cooking a valuable experience, often children can actually help you in the kitchen. Many hands, even if they are small ones, can help with the work.

**Some hints for cooking with children.**

- Make sure you pick a day and a time when you feel calm and relaxed and not particularly worried about the mess or how long a cooking project may take.
- Prepare a work area easily accessible to everyone.
- Strict supervision around heat and sharp utensils is

essential. Explain how these are used and how they might be dangerous if not used in the proper manner.

- Have plenty of smocks and pot holders on hand.
- Extra large bowls (plastic or metal) will prevent spills.
- Have enough mixing spoons to go around.
- Have something for everyone to do if they wish. Young children find it hard to wait for a turn.
- Children all like to take a turn stirring, kneading, and especially tasting the mixture. If possible, have some extra ingredients for smelling and feeling (and spilling).
- Children also love to have you taste what they make, so be prepared to do some tasting yourself.

**Questions to ask in the kitchen.** Where do these foods come from? What foods are good for us? How are they good for us? How does this change when we mix it? Bake it? Freeze it? Is this ingredient soft? Smooth? Grainy? Slippery? Gooey? What does this taste like? What is bigger—this bowl or this cup? What is smaller? What do we need to make salad? What do we need to eat this food we made? And there will be many more questions you never expected!

## FOOD TRIPS IN THE COMMUNITY

Food trips help children discover where the foods they eat come from. Maybe you can see the back of the supermarket where the trucks unload, or pick your own strawberries. Call ahead to arrange a trip that will be thorough. Explain to the children where you are going and what you might see. Following are some possible places to visit:

- An apple orchard
- A downtown open-air market
- A chicken or turkey farm
- A meat market

- A fish market
- A food co-op
- The grocery store or the variety store
- A vegetable stand (especially one that is right next to the field where things are picked)

## SOURCES OF NUTRITION INFORMATION

These organizations have free pamphlets available about nutrition for young children:

1. National Dairy Council, Chicago, Illinois 60606. Look for your local or regional office to request any of these and more.

- "For Good Dental Health, Start Early"
- "Your Child's Health, Day by Day"
- "A Guide to Good Eating" (this may be ordered in notebook, poster, or miniature size; the miniature size comes in Spanish also)
- "Food Before Six"
- "Feeding Little Folks"
- "Feeding Your Baby During His First Year"

2. State Department of Public Health, Nutrition Program. This program distributes booklets, brochures, and information about nutrition.

3. United States Department of Health, Education, and Welfare (HEW), Washington, D.C. 20201.

- Headstart Nutrition Kit is available to associations or groups, and includes booklets on nutrition for young children, a film on nutrition, a ten-lesson course on nutrition for educating parents, and a resource list. Contact your nearby Headstart Program to see if they have these materials for others to look at, and inquire also about any nutrition education courses they might be offering.

Some other HEW publications are available from the United States Department of Health, Education, and Welfare, 5600 Fishers Lane, Rockville, Maryland 20852:

- "Making Mealtimes Happy Times"
- "It's Good Food—Keep It Safe"
- "The Problem Eater"
- "Meals with Tot Appeal"

4. United States Department of Agriculture Food and Nutrition Service, Information Division, Washington, D.C. 20250. The U.S. Department of Agriculture has available many food and nutrition service programs for young children. There are seven regional offices of this department. Contact your regional office by looking in the telephone directory under "U.S. Government."

In addition, the regional chapter of the Home Extension Service, which is a part of the U.S. Department of Agriculture, is a good resource. The Extension Service has a wealth of information and brochures on nutrition, food preparation, canning and freezing procedures, gardening, and the like.

How about having a home economist come from the Extension Service to talk with a group of providers? They are available to plan programs, and there are trained teaching assistants who offer workshops in sewing and batiking, crafts, baking, and home decorating.

5. The nutritionist for the public schools in your town or city will have information and resources concerning nutrition.

6. Homemaker services (and visiting nurse programs) offer trained persons who have experience and knowledge of child care, nutrition, and home management. Look in the yellow pages of the telephone directory for the service near you.

7. Gerber Products Company, 445 State Street, Fremont, Michigan 49412. This baby food company offers the following booklets:

- "Foods for Baby"
- "Mealtime Psychology"

Both of these are free and offer great hints on feeding.

Finally, don't neglect newspapers, magazines, and the cookbook section of your public library for good recipes and tips on nutrition. How about exchanging cookbooks or recipes with other providers? Or collect your own favorite recipes into a looseleaf notebook. Here are some books that family day care providers have suggested:

*Making Your Own Baby Food,* by Mary and James Turner (Bantam Books, New York, 1972). This can be found in many libraries and bookstores and sells for $4.95.

*The Complete Guide to Preparing Baby Foods at Home,* by Sue Castle (Doubleday Publishing Company, Garden City, New York, 1973). This can be found in many libraries and bookstores and costs $5.95.

*Feed Me, I'm Yours,* by Vicky Lansky (Meadowbrook Press, Wayzata, Minnesota, 1974). This is a good cookbook written by mothers for mothers of newborns to five-year-olds.

*The First Baby Cookbook,* by Melinda Morris (Ace Books, New York, 1973).

There are several new cookbooks for cooking with older children, many of which can be read by the children themselves. One family day care provider lets her eleven-year-old read aloud the recipe and show the younger children what to do. This makes the older one feel important, and is good reading practice, too!

*The Mother-Child Cookbook: An Introduction to Educational Cooking,* by Nancy J. Ferreira (Pacific Coast Publishers, Menlo Park, California, 1969).

*Kids Are Natural Cooks,* by Parents Nursery School (Houghton Mifflin, Boston, 1974).

*The Natural Snack Cookbook,* by Jill Pinkwater (Scholastic Book Service, 1975).

*Betty Crocker's Cookbook for Boys and Girls,* by Betty Crocker (Western Publishing, 1975).

## 6. SAFETY

THOUSANDS of children are killed or permanently damaged as a result of household accidents every year. It is vitally important that adults be aware of the possibility of accidents. Making your home as *accident proof* as possible and teaching children about safety really helps save lives.

A child has little clear-cut idea of what is safe; he is curious, and so he explores his surroundings. Babies, it seems, always have something in their mouths. They are trying in the best way they have to understand "what it is." Young children will touch and taste an object to discover "what it's like" and "what it does." Often these explorations involve harmful objects. The young child who has had relatively few experiences with his world is only gradually learning to understand what is safe and what is dangerous. The adult must guide the child towards appreciating the difference, and at the same time must encourage the child to explore. It is a difficult balance to strike.

Safety means something different at each age. It is important to tailor rules about dangerous objects to the age of the child and to his understanding. Fours and fives can write with sharp pencils, but babies and toddlers will probably put them in their mouths. Lots of explaining what is safe and how to use things, lots of understanding and basic trust in the child, and an acceptance of some anxious moments, are all part of learning about safety.

Mrs. F. says she teaches the older children how to handle emergencies in case she is immobilized. She has set up a hierarchy with the older kids and trained them to cope with an emergency that involves her. In order to get them used to the idea of coping, she might pretend to take half an hour off for a cup of coffee at a neighbor's (she can watch from the window and see how things are going). Or she and the older children could practice what they do in an emergency. (Of course, you should never leave a younger child alone in any circumstances.)

Mrs. S. called the fire department and rescue squad to ask them to explain procedures for emergencies to her; the fire department came for a visit to explain in person!

## MAKING THE HOME SAFE FOR CHILDREN

There are several steps you can take to make your home safer:

- Put a list of emergency numbers by the phone. Include the doctor, ambulance, rescue squad, fire department, police, and poison control center. You might want to put the emergency numbers for each child in your care here, too (their doctors, parents, and person to call if the parent can't be reached; you should also have signed permission slips for emergency care).

*Teach yng child to dial phone*

- Have a first-aid kit or supplies readily available.
- Be sure you know where the children are at all times. Stay within hearing. ("If there's silence in the next room, you can be sure I go in to see what's causing it!" a provider says.)
- Read the labels on any household paint to make sure there's no lead in it. You can ask a person to come from the local health department and check your house for dangerous lead paint. Lead is poisonous and some children may put peeling paint chips in their mouths.
- Sharp objects (knives, nails, pins, fingernail files, and such) are best stored out of reach of small hands. If a child does find them, explain how dangerous they are.
- Choking is common among small children, especially babies who will put anything in their mouths. Be particularly watchful that small objects such as buttons, beads, pins, or even small candies are out of reach. If choking does occur, reach inside the child's mouth and try to remove the obstruction. Then turn the child upside-down and slap sharply several times between the shoulder blades.
- Never leave a child in the bathtub or wading pool alone, even for a moment. It's possible to drown in only an inch or two of water; better to let the phone ring than to have a tragedy occur.
- Be aware that unused refrigerators and freezers are a terrible hazard for children, who can become trapped inside them and suffocate. The law requires that doors be removed from such appliances when they are not in use.
- Store all medicines out of children's reach on a high shelf or in a locked cupboard. Some medicines have child-proof caps that are so effective even you will have a hard time getting them off!
- Always read the label before giving a child medicine.
- Turn pot handles away from the front of the stove.

- High chairs tip easily; if you have one, make sure it has a broad base or place it next to a wall. If you pile up cushions or books on chairs for the little ones, check them often to be sure they are sturdy. Low chair and table sets are a good combination. They can be made simply and very inexpensively.
- Broken toys are a menace in play areas; if they are beyond repair, toss them out!
- Broken glass and opened cans are best put in a tightly covered receptacle.
- Upstairs windows need guards. A good safety practice is to open them only at the top.
- Going up and down stairs can be a hassle if the stairs are not in good repair; a sturdy handrail helps.
- To avoid electric shocks, keep cords in good condition. Electrical outlets that are not used should be covered up with plug locks (found at hardware stores and supermarkets) or with masking tape.
- Door stops and safety knobs will keep children from opening doors to places where they are not supposed to go.
- Matches should be kept out of reach so as not to tempt small hands.
- Styrofoam can be exceedingly dangerous. If it is swallowed or inhaled it is undetectable by X ray, and the child must have exploratory surgery.
- Keep closet doors shut and make sure children don't go into them to play. A child can quickly suffocate in dry cleaner's plastic or other plastic bags. (When you discard dry cleaner's plastic, be sure to tie it into knots before putting it in the wastebasket, so that a curious baby doesn't get into it.)
- Beans and seeds that are used for collages or other projects are best kept out of baby's and toddler's grasp. When these are placed in ears or noses or swallowed they can swell and be very painful.
- Flush old medicines down the toilet.

- Cleaning materials, polish, dishwashing detergents, paint thinner, hairwaving lotions, boric acid solutions, weed killers, and ammonia must be kept out of small hands' reach. If a child swallows poison, call the rescue squad and the poison control center *immediately* and follow any directions for remedies that are given on the container. When you go to the hospital, take the poison container with you.
- Tablecloths that hang over the edge of a table can be pulled off and are dangerous—things may fall on the child's head.
- When serving a hot meal or beverage put the container in the middle of the table.
- When cooking, be aware that something might spill, splatter, or tip on a baby or small child in the kitchen area.

**Resources for household safety and emergencies.** As well as having emergency numbers posted by your phone, it is a good idea to have a basic reference shelf for health matters. There are several good children's medical encyclopedias available in bookstores. And in order to know more about safety and emergency procedures in the home, you might send for some of the following free booklets.

- "Accident Handbook" is a booklet available from the Children's Hospital Medical Center, Department of Health Education, 300 Longwood Avenue, Boston, Massachusetts 02215. It suggests ways to prevent children's accidents and ways to treat various types of accidents when they occur.
- "Young Children and Accidents in the Home" is a pamphlet by the U.S. Department of Health, Education, and Welfare (#014E) and is available free from the Consumer Information Center, Pueblo, Colorado 81009.
- "American Red Cross First Aid Textbook" is available from your local chapter of the Red Cross. There

is much information on safety for children and adults.

- "First Aid for the Family," by the Metropolitan Life Insurance Company, is available from the MLIC, Health and Welfare Division, P.O. Box 1, One Madison Avenue, New York, New York 10010 (or contact the local office in your area). This is a reference card on common first-air procedures and mouth-to-mouth breathing. The same company can send you a useful pamphlet on home safety, called "Your Child's Safety."
- "First Aid Manual," by the American Medical Association (AMA), is available from the AMA, 535 North Dearborn Street, Chicago, Illinois 60610. This booklet describes how to control bleeding, maintain breathing, and prevent shock after injury.
- "Your Child and Household Safety," by the American Academy of Pediatrics, Accident Prevention Committee, 1801 Hinman Avenue, P.O. Box 1034, Evanston, Illinois 60204.

*Fire safety.* Local fire companies often have brochures to hand out, especially during fire safety weeks. Ask them for a reflective red decal called a "tot finder" to identify a child's room to the firemen.

- "Fire Safety Code for Day Care Homes," by the Life Safety Code, is available from the National Fire Protection Association, 470 Atlantic Avenue, Boston, Massachusetts 02110. Ask for other related free publications.

*Poisoning.*

- *Poison Control Center:* Check in your phone book for a listing of the local poison control center; hospitals and clinics often have a center, or they can direct you to one. Most poison centers are open 24 hours. For information on different types of poisonous substances and possible treatments, send for brochures from the National Safety Council, 425 North Michigan Avenue, Chicago, Illinois 60611.

- For information on lead poisoning, request pamphlet number 2108-1970 from the Superintendent of Documents, U.S. Government Printing Office, Washington, D.C. 20402.
- *Poisonous plants* are common, even in the home. Did you know that poinsettia leaves are so lethal that one leaf can kill a child? Or that mistletoe berries have proved fatal to both children and adults who have eaten them? There are plants that are harmful, or even fatal—and it's a good idea to know which ones. There is a free chart of poisonous plants available from Geigy Chemical Company, Saw Mill River Road, Ardsley, New York 10502. Also, some plant stores will have leaflets describing poisonous plants.

*Toy safety.* Many toys have been proved harmful to children. There is a federal law (#91-113) that allows a government agency to take unsafe toys off the shelves and allows you to get your money back on any toys you can prove are hazardous.

- Consumer Information on Toys is a group that has free booklets on toy safety and crib safety, and even a banned toy list. This information is available from the Public Documents Distribution Center, Pueblo, Colorado 81008. These people can also send you a complete listing of consumer publications upon request.
- U.S. Consumer Product Safety Commissions, 1750 K Street N.W., Washington, D.C. 20207. Ask these people for materials on common toy hazards, children's coloring books on toy safety, and any other information on toy safety. They have the following publications:
  "Toy Safety: Always in Season" (CPSC Pub. No. 6302-74)

"Crib Safety: Keep Them on the Safe Side" (CPSC Pub. No. 6305-74)
- Superintendent of Documents, U.S. Government Printing Office, Washington, D.C. 20402.
"Toy Safety" (No. 73-7009)
"Playing Safe in Toyland" (No. 72-7018)
"Safe Use of Children's Toys" (No. 73-7014)
- *Toys That Don't Care,* by Edward Schwartz, is a book about the dangerous toys manufactured for young children. Ask for this book at your library.

## TRANSPORTING CHILDREN SAFELY

When going on a trip with young children it is important to take some safety precautions. Preparing yourself and the children really helps make the trip run more smoothly.

One family day care provider says that she tries to bring along another adult when she goes places far from the house. Sometimes she teams up with another provider and they all go together. That way, if a crisis should come up one adult can take care of it while the other sees to the rest of the children.

Whether you are going across town or just around the block, some talking to the children in advance is very helpful. Explain where you are going and remind them of some of the behavior you will expect of them—holding hands while crossing streets, looking both ways before crossing, not running ahead too far, and so on. It helps them to know what to expect on the trip.

If they will need to sit still for a while in a bus or car, prepare them. If the trip involves a lot of "sit quietly" time, Mrs. Y. brings along some things to help her children stay still, such as a game, a doll, or a favorite teddy bear.

Even on a short trip you can always count on making at least one visit to the toilet or drinking fountain. If possible, try to find out beforehand where these are located.

Trips can even be overstimulating for children and excite them too much. Try simple ones at first—not too far from home.

**Bike safety.** Did you know that the bicycle ranks number one on the Consumer Product Safety Commission's list of dangerous household products? Be sure your day care children have structurally sound trikes and bikes that fit them, and that they know some basic safety rules for riding. Information and free materials on bike safety are available from the U.S. Consumer Product Safety Commission, Washington, D.C. 20207.

If you carry children in bike seats on your own bicycle, be sure to use a seat that receives a good rating from the Consumers' Union. These include (by make and number) AMF #C45, Sears #48523, Troxel #4, and Ward's #82657. Others may have been approved since the printing of this book, so write to the U.S. Consumer Product Safety Commission (address above) for an up-to-date listing.

**Car safety.** Children need special protection when riding in a car. Standard safety belts are not considered safe for children under four years of age (or less than 40 pounds in weight) because seat belts exert too much pressure on the abdominal area and could cause injury in a crash. Consumer Reports recommends several types of car restraints for children.

- General Motors Infant Seat (for children up to 20 pounds); available at Buick, Chevrolet, Oldsmobile, Pontiac, and Cadillac dealers. Note: this seat can be used around the house as an infant seat.
- Ford Tot Guard (up to 50 pounds); available at Ford dealers.
- General Motors Love Seat (up to 40 pounds); available at G.M. dealers.
- Sears Child Safety Harness (check for weight limits with Sears); available from the Sears Catalogue, No. 28A6401.

- Bobby Mac (up to 35 pounds); available from the Collier Keyworth Company. Note: earlier models of this seat were not adequately crash-proof. Make sure to purchase a shield (sold separately) to get maximum protection if you buy a used one.
- Peterson Model 74 or 75 (up to 50 pounds); available from the Peterson Company. These are the only recommended models made by this company.
- Kentworth Car Seat, Models 884 and 784 (up to 45 pounds); available from the Kentworth Company. These are the only recommended seats made by this company.

Car seats are a vital part of car safety for children, but they are expensive. Look for used car seats before you buy new models, since children rapidly grow out of them. Thrift stores, yard sales, and other providers may be some good sources for finding good used car seats.

For more information write to Action for Child Transportation Safety (ACTS), 400 Central Park West, No. 15-P, New York, New York 10025. This organization has information concerning transportation safety.

## CHILD ABUSE AND NEGLECT

Too many children in our society are permanently damaged by abuse and neglect. It is not pleasant to think about, but it is a reality that many of us will come face to face with. Day care providers, who are in close contact with young children, often may observe signs of abuse and neglect. Family day care providers, because they have contact with both the child and the parent, may be able to help the family deal with this problem.

**Signs of abuse and neglect.** These are the most common warning signs of child abuse or neglect:

- The child has more cuts, bruises, bites, burns, welts, and other injuries than is usual. Parents may be reluctant to explain these "accidents" when asked.

- The child is constantly tired, apathetic, and withdrawn.
- The child appears undernourished.
- The child wears dirty, torn clothes and is in need of a good scrubbing.
- The child needs medical attention.
- The child's parents describe him or her as "bad" or "different" from other children.

**You can help.** In thinking about possible abuse or neglect it is important to use your common sense. Try to talk with the parents and find out what is happening. The parents may need information or help from other adults. Try not to be judgmental. Be helpful.

A day care provider has a responsibility to the child and to the parents to report a suspected case of child abuse or neglect. (This is the law.) This report may be made by telephone, but later you may be asked to submit something in writing, as documentation is very important.

A person who reports child abuse will be helping not only the child but the parents as well. The child will get medical attention, and the parents will get counseling to prevent the abuse from continuing. Social agencies that deal with abuse and neglect try to keep families together, if possible, and to counsel the parents. This is a long-term procedure.

**Resources for abuse and neglect problems.** A national organization called Parents Anonymous staffs a free and confidential telephone hotline service. If you have a child in your home you suspect is being abused or neglected, let the parent know about Parents Anonymous. This is a group of concerned parents who admit to expressing their difficulties with their children through physical or verbal abuse. They provide self-help and support groups to help each other deal with this problem. They meet weekly without a therapist for discussion, and they exchange phone numbers so they can call one another when they need support. For information about the chapter nearest you, write:

- Parents Anonymous, 2930 West Imperial Highway, Suite 332, Inglewood, California 90303; or
- Parents Anonymous, Incorporated, 250 West 57th Street, Room 1901, New York, New York 10019.

Each state has an office that is responsible for handling child abuse and neglect cases. This agency is usually referred to as the children's protective services, and is most often administered by the department of welfare or by a special state department for children's services. Look in your telephone book under the state government. Many newspapers also have an "800" telephone number to call within the state for help with child abuse and neglect cases. And very often organizations that work with children will have workshops or conferences on this topic.

Another organization that has publications and information is the National Committee for the Prevention of Child Abuse, 836 West Wellington Avenue, Chicago, Illinois 60657.

A free reading list on abuse and neglect has been prepared by the National Institute of Mental Health. Send for DHEW Publication No. (HSM) 73-9034, available from the U.S. Department of HEW, Public Health Service, Alcohol, Drug Abuse, and Mental Health Administration, 5600 Fishers Lane, Rockville, Maryland 20852.

A free pamphlet on child abuse and neglect, called "Children at Risk," is available from the Day Care Council of New York, 114 East 32nd Street, New York, New York 10016.

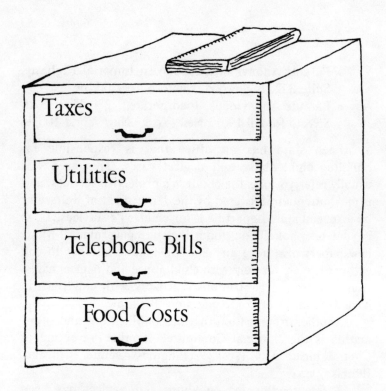

## 7. KEEPING RECORDS

WHEN YOU USE YOUR HOME for day care, there are
some things you will need to know about keeping records.
Family day care is considered to be a business in your home,
so you can expect to have a certain amount of paperwork. It
would be advantageous to think beforehand about the
kinds of records you keep, and to organize them in a
systematic way that works for you.

Many providers find it useful to keep a small file
system that includes a folder for each child, one for the
forms required for licensing, and folders on any additional
information that might be needed. Many providers keep a
folder of correspondence (letters to parents and to agencies
concerned with children's services). Mrs. D. keeps her
business paperwork in a large cardboard storage box she
got on sale at the local drugstore. File folders just fit in the
box and there is plenty of room for all her information.

You will also need to devise a method for keeping track of the financial end of your family day care business. You will need attendance sheets, records of fee payments by parents, and an itemized account of what you spend for the day care business.

## TAX MATTERS

In the eyes of the income tax people (Internal Revenue Service) you have a private business in your home, if you are operating independently. As a working person, you must declare your earnings as income. Since your principal place of business is your home (that's where you do your work), you are able to claim some deductions from your earnings, which might be to your advantage. You will fill out Schedule C (along with Form 1040) if you are the sole owner of your family day care business. A sample of this form is included as an Appendix to this book.

Should you claim deductions? Some people do not need to. If the family income (including your earnings) is very low, so that there is no income tax due, then it is probably not to your advantage to figure out all of the permissible deductions. But if the combined family income is at a level where it is taxed (this is where most of us are), it is to your advantage to calculate all permissible deductions and, by doing this, reduce the income tax you owe.

Deductions generally fall into two categories: direct expenses and indirect expenses. You may deduct both types of expenses to the extent that they are ordinary and necessary to your business.

**Deductions for direct expenses.** Direct expenses are those such as the cost of food, toys, supplies, and anything else used for day care children in your home; the cost of advertisements, if any, which you have placed in local papers; safety devices (socket covers, fire extinguishers, and so on); extra beds, cots, cribs, or bedding; a license to operate; office supplies; or anything else you need to conduct your business. It is not necessary to keep a record of all expenses for the year down to the last penny for your tax return. It is necessary, though, to justify the deductions.

A record of what was spent in a week for food for your day care children would be enough evidence for the tax people. Your list might look like this:

*Items Bought for Feeding Children Breakfast, Lunch, and Snacks, Week of May 1, 1979*

| | |
|---|---:|
| 3 loaves of bread at $.66 per loaf | $1.98 |
| 1 box of cereal at $1.15 per box | 1.15 |
| 2 lbs. of cheese at $2.09 per lb. | 4.18 |
| 3 cans of soup at $.31 per can | .93 |
| 1½ gallons of milk at $.90 per ½ gallon | 2.70 |
| 3 cans of applesauce at $.44 per can | 1.32 |
| 3 lbs. of grapefruit at $.25 per lb. | .75 |
| 1 box of crackers at $.79 | .79 |
| 1 carton of eggs at $.88 | .88 |
| 1 lb. of peanut butter at $1.05 | 1.05 |
| 1 head of lettuce at $.59 | .59 |
| 1 jar of mayonnaise at $1.13 | 1.13 |
| TOTAL | $17.45 |

A quick way to figure out the yearly food costs for your day care children from a weekly list like this is as follows:

1. Figure out the cost per child per week (divide the total food bill by the number of children).
2. Figure out the number of weeks of care for each child, and then add these numbers together to find the total of "child-weeks" for the year.
3. Multiply the cost per child (from step 1) by the total of child-weeks (from step 2) to arrive at the yearly cost.

For example, if the total extra food bill comes to $15.00 for the week and you have three day care children who come to your house, then the cost per child per week is $5.00 ($15.00 ÷ 3 = $5.00). If these children were in your care for 42, 43, and 45 weeks respectively during the year, then the total of child-weeks is 130 (42 + 43 + 45 = 130). If you multiply $5.00 (cost per child per week) by 130 (number of child-weeks) you get $650—which is the approximate amount that you spent for food for the day care children for a year.

Records for other direct expenses, such as cribs and toys, are easily kept if you have the actual receipts for buying them. (It helps to note on the receipt what was bought, if it is not already noted, so that you will remember which is for what.) If you don't have receipts, you can cut out newspaper ads that show what you bought and for how much.

Mrs. A. has a method of record-keeping she calls the "shoebox method." She collects all records of her expenses (weekly food receipts, receipts for materials and equipment purchased for day care, canceled checks or similar evidence of payments) in a shoebox which she keeps on her "business shelf" above the phone. She has one shoebox for each year, starting a new one each January 1st. Since it is a good idea to have three years of expenses on record in the event of a tax audit (rare, but it could happen), Mrs. A. keeps the boxes for three years before tossing them out.

You can also deduct educational expenses (fees for courses related to your work, and the cost of materials for such educational programs) if you attend courses, workshops, or conferences that are related to your profession of child care. Keep your receipts for any fees you pay.

**Deductions for indirect expenses.** Indirect expenses are those involving the use of your house for day care. You can deduct a portion of the household expenses, such as mortgage interest, property taxes, rent, telephone, utilities, maintenance, and wear and tear on the house.

First, you need to find out what portion of the total household expenses can be attributed to the day care business. If the entire house is available for day care and is used by the children for half of the day (approximately twelve hours), then you may deduct half of the utility bills and the rent or mortgage payments.

If only a few rooms are used for day care half of the day, there are two ways to figure out the deductible portion:

1. Figure out what proportion of the rooms in the house are used for day care. Mrs. D. has nine rooms in her house and she uses three for day care; thus, she uses 3/9, or 1/3, of the house for her business. Since this part is used for only half the day, she must divide 1/3 by 2, which equals 1/6. So one-sixth of her household expenses may be deducted.

2. Figure out the square footage of the space used for day care and express this figure as a percentage of the total amount of space in the house. This is a more exact method. Mrs. D., who uses three of her nine rooms for day care, got out her tape measure and found that the three rooms contained 540 square feet (multiply the length of the room by the width to get the area in square feet). The entire house contains 1,640 square feet. She divides 540 by 1,640 and gets .33—that is, 33 percent, or one-third, of the house is used for day care. (Note that this is the same answer arrived at by the rougher method above.) Because she uses one-third of the house for half the day, she may deduct one-sixth of her household expenses.

In order for Mrs. D. to figure out her actual deduction, she must now multiply the deductible fraction or percentage by her actual expenditures for rent, gas, electricity, and so on. If her gas bill for the month is $12, then her deduction would be 1/6 times $12, or $2 per month.

Another indirect expense is the telephone bill. The time that the phone is in use or is needed for the day care business is deductible. If you care for children for half the day (twelve hours) then you may deduct up to half of the monthly service charge. A tax consultant can give you more information on this.

The "wear and tear" on your home is another deductible indirect expense. If the home is owned by you it may be advantageous to calculate this deduction. This is how to do it:

You need to know the *current value* of the house (without the land, as the land will not depreciate in value). A recent property tax statement may be used as evidence. If the assessment of property in your community is made at the rate of, say, 50 percent, this means that the assessed value of the home is 50 percent (or one half) of the actual value. So, if Mrs. D.'s home is assessed at $8,000 and her land at $2,000 at a 50 percent rate, she will then figure the current value of her house at twice $8,000, which is $16,000.

Because her day care business uses one-sixth of the house, the *base for wear and tear* is one-sixth of the current value—or 1/6 times $16,000, which is $2,667.

Next, you need to figure out how long this wear and tear will go on. The *useful life* of a property is the number of years that family day care will be done in the home. Mrs. D. plans to continue to take in day care children for at least ten years, until her own children are finished with high school. The useful life of her house is, therefore, ten years.

You must now figure out how much your day care space will be worth at the end of its useful life. To do this, you must look first at the current value of similar houses that are as old as yours will be when you stop providing day care. Mrs. D. looks at the current value of homes like hers, but ten years older. She can ask a real estate broker or tax consultant, or look at the real estate ads in the newspaper. In her case, she finds that her home will probably be worth the equivalent of $12,000 in ten years.

In ten years, then, the space Mrs. D. uses for day care (one-sixth of her house) will be worth one-sixth of $12,000, or $2,000. This $2,000 is called the *salvage value*.

Now, armed with the base for wear and tear, the useful life, and the salvage value, she can figure a yearly wear and tear deduction. Mrs. D. has a base for wear and tear of $2,667, a useful life of ten years, and a salvage value of $2,000.

| | |
|---|---:|
| The base for wear and tear | $2,667 |
| Minus the salvage value in ten years | −2,000 |
| Nets the wear and tear for ten years | $  667 |
| The yearly wear and tear for ten years | $667.00 |
| Divided by the useful life of ten years | ÷ 10 |
| Nets the yearly deduction | $  66.70 |

Mrs. D. may deduct $66.70 per year for wear and tear on her house. It seems like a lot of figuring for that amount, but every bit counts!

**Social Security tax.** Your income is subject to self-employment Social Security payments. This payment is figured on Form 1040, Schedule SE, at the time your income tax is filed. It may be easier to pay this once a year than to do it quarterly (there is no profit in paying it quarterly anyway). Christmas club savings accounts are one way of putting the money aside so you'll be sure to have it at tax time.

**Resources for tax matters.** This tax business can be really confusing, and there are people who can help you with it. The local Internal Revenue Service (IRS) office, a tax consultant or attorney, or a legal aid office can help you fill out the forms and figure out your deductions.

This is also a pamphlet by Eva C. Galambos called "Income Tax Deductions for Family Day Care Homes," available from EDRS, Leasco Information Products, Inc., P.O. Drawer O, Bethesda, Maryland 20014. The number of the publication is ED 060955.

H. & R. Block and Company puts out an annual income tax workbook that gives step-by-step instructions for preparing your returns. There is usually a sample form for a home business of some kind, and this can be very helpful for family day care providers.

## INSURANCE

Obtaining the proper insurance to cover your family day care activities can be a confusing and frustrating process—but it is absolutely necessary that you do so. You must be financially protected from the consequences of accidents that occur on your premises. If a child falls off a swing and is badly injured while in your care, the parents are within their legal rights to press claims against you for negligence—even if there was no way that you could have prevented the accident.

Your insurance policy should protect you against liability for: 1) Bodily injury that occurs accidentally; 2) Accidental damage to the property of another; 3) Expenses of immediate medical relief at the time of the accident; and 4) The legal costs of defending against suits by injured parties.

The least complicated way to obtain such insurance is to attach a "rider" to your existing homeowner's policy. (If you rent your home, you should carry a tenant's insurance policy. Be certain that the insurance agent understands that the rider is specifically for family day care (or "home child care")—*not* for a "day care center" or a "nursery school." There is a big difference in how insurance companies regard these things, and the simpler you can keep it, the better off you will be.

Many state family day care associations or child care councils offer insurance policies for family day care operations. If yours does not, this is something that an association of independent providers could work together to obtain. Check with your licensing authority about this.

If you will be transporting children anywhere in your car, make sure your automobile insurance policy covers you to a generous degree. It is well worth increasing your coverage, if you now carry only what is required by law. There is no situation in which the risk is greater and the potential loss is higher.

Finally, you should know that whatever insurance premiums you pay to cover your family day care operations are completely tax deductible.

# 8. WORKING WITH PARENTS

IN ARRANGING TO PROVIDE CARE for a child, there is much information to be exchanged between you and the parent. A visit is helpful for you, the child, and the parent.

The visit is a time for meeting the child and parent and seeing how they get along. Even in a brief visit you can pick up clues. For their part, the child and parent can meet you and become familiar with your home ahead of time. The child can meet the other children you care for, and you can see how a new child might fit in with the others.

Mrs. D. has the parent(s) and the child come for the first interview. "We talk about the home, what I do in an emergency, what I charge, and business details; also how I discipline, and anything else that might come up. Then I ask the parent to tell the child she is leaving, but that she will be back very soon. She then leaves my home for a cup of coffee or a long walk around the block, and comes back a half hour later. That is a short enough time for the child to see that she *will* return. It's important that the child believe that the parent will return, in my book."

## GETTING TO KNOW THE CHILD

Parents can provide you with most of the essential information about their child. You might ask about:

- Eating habits. What are the child's likes and dislikes; what are his or her favorite foods? Explain what type of meals you provide and give a sample menu, if possible.
- Sleeping habits. Does the child nap? For how long? At what time?
- Play activities. What are the child's favorite games and toys? What sort of things does the parent do to have fun with the child? To ease the child out of uncomfortable times?
- Trips. How does the parent feel about your taking the child out? In your car? A bus? A train? How does the parent feel about the child playing outdoors in cold weather? In storms? If you go outdoors with the children, ask that each child be dressed appropriately for the season and weather.
- Toilet habits. If the child is old enough, is he or she trained? If you are to help with the training, do you and the parent have similar ideas? Do you have an understanding of each other's toilet training techniques?
- Discipline. Do you and the parent have a similar approach to discipline? When and how does the parent punish? Do you and the parent agree (as much as is possible, for everyone has different ideas) so that the child doesn't have to deal with two very different disciplinarians? How do you and the parent handle temper tantrums or behavior that disrupts others?

- Health. Does the child have any known health problems? What is being done, if anything? Will the parent keep you informed on the health situation?

**A period of adjustment.** Many providers have what they call a period of adjustment when they take on a new child. This may be about two weeks or so, in which the day care arrangement is still considered temporary.

The provider watches how the child fits into the home. Is he happy? Let the parent know about the adjustment process of the child.

If the situation doesn't seem to be working out, it is the provider's responsibility to let the parent know—perhaps another type of day care arrangement is in order. *This isn't a failure.*

During the adjustment period it helps the child to bring along a favorite thing from home (a teddy bear, blanket, toy, or perhaps a key chain with a key on it that the parent doesn't need). This helps to make the transition from the family home to your home smoother. Something familiar to clutch and tie you to home base when your world is a bit uncertain sure helps!


## WHAT DO YOU DO IF . . . ?

Some emergency measures should be worked out between you and the parents whenever you make a child care arrangement. What do you do if an accident or an emergency occurs? Some day care providers will explain to the parents in detail what steps they will take.

There is certain information you need for emergencies and illnesses. Ask the parent to provide a sheet with the names, addresses, and telephone numbers of parents, friends, or relatives to call in an emergency, as well as the child's doctor. You should also get a signed emergency release form so that you can seek medical care for the child if necessary.

**Illness.** You might check with the parents about these points:

- Should you contact the parent at work if the child has a fever?
- Will you take a child who has a bad cold?
- How about agreeing to tell the parent if any illness occurs in the home among the other children (mumps, measles, and so on)?
- What if you get sick? (That's never supposed to happen, of course.) Will you offer a substitute?
- Can you give medicines (prescribed or otherwise) to the child? How about aspirin?
- What allergies (if any) does the child have?

There is helpful information on allergies and how to reduce environmental irritants in the *Parents Yellow Pages,* a book by the Princeton Center for Infancy (Anchor Books, New York; 1978).

## FEES AND OTHER BUSINESS DETAILS

Explain clearly to the parent what you charge for child care. You might want to consider a reduced or sliding scale for a family with more than one child in your home.

It is important, however, not to price yourself out of business because of sheer kindness. You are working extremely hard and providing an invaluable service for children and parents. Yours is a professional role and it is important that you be paid accordingly.

Some information a parent would like to know might be:

- What does your fee include? Will you supply lunch, as well as snacks? Or should the parent supply it? How about lunch money for special trips? Or fees and fares for trips?
- What are the hours of care?
- How strictly do you hold to these times?

- When is the fee due? If the parent is just starting a new job, will you make an allowance for payment of the fee in the first month or two?
- How about vacation time? What about the days of a parent's vacation? Will you charge even though the child is not there? Will you hold a place for a child on a parent's vacation?
- When you take a vacation, will you suggest another home or substitute while you are away?
- Do you offer any special types of care? Overnight? Weekends?
- What will the children call you? "Mom"? "Mrs. ———"? "Aunt ———"? Or by your first name?

In addition, you will have practical details to discuss with the parent:

- When will the child arrive? When is pick-up time? Will it vary or change? Let the parent know *your* needs. If your own family is tired and hungry by 6 p.m. and screaming for supper, tell the parent this and ask that she be prompt.
- If a public agency is paying for day care, find out how it pays (the rate-setting agreement). Try to find out beforehand, if possible, if this agency is generally late in paying and when you might expect the fee to be paid. Often state agencies are a few months behind in payments, and it helps to know this in advance.
- Who will pick up the child? Most providers prefer that the person who is picking up a child in their care come in at the time of pick-up. Important information about the child's day is usually exchanged at this time, and it is best done face to face.

    Mrs. A. has a signature list of those persons designated by the parents to pick up the child. The list is in Mrs. A.'s hands before the first day of care. After all, she says, "I can't have just any person waltz in off the street and pick up my children." Mrs. E.

insists on meeting each of the persons who might pick up a child in her home. "I feel a lot better about seeing someone face-to-face, and then I know it's okay that they take the child home." These are all ways of being sure that the child is all right going home with persons other than the parents; it assures you, if no one else.

## CONTINUING COMMUNICATION WITH PARENTS

In order to work together as well as possible for the good of the child, open communication between you and the parent is very important. After all, neither of you can do your job well without the other.

You are the one who calls the children "my children" or "my day care children," cares for them, feeds them, helps snap up trousers, buttons, and dresses, ties their shoes, wipes runny noses, bandages scraped knees, and comforts them. You are "just like Mom or Dad," but you are not actually them. The children do have parents and this needs to be respected. To make the bridge between the parents and you as comfortable as possible, it is necessary to *share the care.*

**Separation problems.** Parents have mixed feelings about separating from their children. They sometimes might feel a little jealous of the provider, who gets to have their child all day—especially when the child cries when it's time to leave the day care home, or even calls the provider "Mommy."

Mrs. F. remembers an incident where the parent really took action when her baby "seemed unhappy." The baby always cried when leaving her home. The mother was upset, and put the baby into another day care arrangement. The problem may never have been really solved. The baby cried because it was being separated from someone with whom it had formed an attachment; but the mother misinterpreted it to be a cry of unhappiness with that particular home. In fact it is good for a baby to have a relationship with another adult, and it is important to think of the child and not just the adults in such situations and then to talk about it.

There are ways to help both the child and the parent with separations:

- Talk with the child: reassure him or her that the parent will be back at the expected hour.
- A phone call sometimes helps, or some other connection with the parent. Encourage the parent to call and ask if everything is okay. If the child needs it and won't completely fall apart, let him or her talk with the parent.
- Have the parent leave a phone number handy so that the child is aware that Mom is only a few numbers away.
- Try putting up a picture of the parent(s) at the child's eye level. The child can point to the picture and talk about the parent.
- Talk with all your day care parents as much as you can at the end of the day. Mrs. F. says she enjoys being with adult company after spending so much time with the children. She tries to talk with each parent at least once a week about her child.

It's not necessary to talk just about family upsets, or even just the child. How about sharing recipes, operations, good restaurants, work-related issues, common professional interests, anything?

**Sensitive issues.** Some issues are more sensitive than others. Knowing how parents might feel about controversial topics helps you communicate clearly to the child how he or she might deal with them. How do you and the parents feel about such things as:

- Toilet training
- Sex-related questions
- Death, birth, divorce, separation, marriage
- Religion

- Holidays
- Table manners, rules for socializing
- Ways of dealing with conflict, fighting, discipline?

If a parent requests that you spank a child when he misbehaves, and you have never spanked a child before, how can you two work this out? Arriving at a clear understanding of what role you play in the area of discipline helps. You are *not* the parent and cannot be expected to do exactly as the parent does. At the start, explain to the parents how you handle problems that arise—this gives you an opportunity to share with parents knowledge that may be helpful to them. It is also asking them for their thoughts and advice, making them feel important in sharing the care.

Sometimes, however, a parent will ask you for some specific help on how to handle a child's behavior problem. You can explain what works for you in that particular situation, and you can direct the parent to some easy reading. You may want to have some pamphlets available to lend to parents. Here are some helpful booklets to send for:

- *A Guide to Discipline* by Jeannette Galambos Stone, available from NAEYC Publications, 1834 Connecticut Avenue NW, Washington, D.C. 20009.
- Available from Ross Laboratories, Columbus, Ohio 43216 are
  "Your Child's Fears"
  "When Your Child Is Unruly"
  "When Your Child Is Contrary"
  "Your Children's Quarrels"

**Setting limits.** It's hard to do, but sometimes it is necessary to say "No" to a parent. Mrs. C. says that once she felt "taken advantage of" by a parent. The agreed pick-up time for her child was 6 p.m. When the mother didn't arrive until 6:15 p.m. and then one night 6:30 p.m., Mrs. C. didn't say anything. The mother mentioned something about traffic. Soon 6:30 became the usual time for the mother to arrive, and toward the end of the week it got later and later. Mrs. C. explained that she had things to do for her own family and that the mother must pick up her child by 6 p.m. or call her if it was going to be later. The mother agreed, but continued to arrive late. Finally, one Friday evening Mrs. C. had to go out at 7:30, and the child was still there! "When the mother came in at 7:45, I told her that this was too much—I felt that I was being 'taken' and the day care arrangement would have to end."

A day care arrangement that is successful must fulfill the needs of all persons involved—the children, the parents, and you. Don't be afraid to state your case and say "No."

Mrs. S. says she learned how to say no when a day care arrangement was not going well:

> I had a baby that I was taking care of. For the first week, the mother brought the baby, a change of clothes, and Pampers, faithfully. Then the next week she brought only the baby and the clothes. I used my own supply of Pampers and didn't say anything—she probably forgot or couldn't get to a store. Well, the days went on and still she brought no Pampers. I was getting sick of this and running out of extra Pampers. So one day when I saw her coming up the walk with her baby I met her at the door (with screwed-up courage) and announced, "No Pampers, no baby!" And I held firm. She went right out to the store and bought some. She has kept me in good supply ever since, and now we can laugh about it.

Whether it is a parent being tardy in picking up a child or the fact that a particular child is not appropriate for your program or whatever, the situation can often be such that you must remember your rights and feelings and talk about them.

At the end of this book I have included sample forms and letters that you can use in working with parents to exchange the information you both need.

# 9. SHARING
# WITH OTHER PROVIDERS

HOW ABOUT FORMING a group of family day care providers? A group offers the chance to get together with other providers to chat, exchange ideas, plan events, and solve problems. A cohesive organization can also exert some force upon the community and make known the providers' needs.

There are numerous advantages to forming such a group. "For one, it breaks down the isolation of being your home," says one provider. "I really value the emotional support," remarks another. Some groups have started toy loans, formed food coops, discussed the rights and responsibilities of parents and providers, and thought about the status of family day care providers in the community.

If you decide to seek out others in your situation to

start a group, the state licensing worker might be able to give you names and addresses of providers in your area. Her office could also advise you on how other groups have formed and what they have done.

In thinking about a place to meet, try to locate a central spot. The home of a member could provide a cozy atmosphere, or there are public places that are available for meetings. Churches, Rotary clubs, Lions clubs, town halls, civic groups, and savings and loan associations are usually willing to donate some space if they have the facilities.

Get in touch personally with providers who are interested by telephoning or visiting them, and let them know where you will meet, when, and how to get there.

In making an agenda of what to accomplish, simple tasks are the easiest to try first. Exchanging ideas on activities for a snowy day, setting up toy loans, having a rummage or bake sale, discussing questions of discipline, teaming up with two or three homes to go to the zoo—these are all possible places to start. You might have a discussion of safe toys, for instance. Request a discussion guide from the Consumer Product Safety Commission, 1750 K Street NW, Washington, D.C. 20207.

Contact a local high school or college for baby-sitters while you meet if you need it for the evening.

But don't expect a huge showing at first. Attendance may be sporadic. After providing care for long hours, many providers can't always make it out at night, too. These things take time to get off the ground. You may need to arrange car pools among yourselves.


## FOOD COOPS

A food coop is people cooperatively buying food in bulk and distributing it, in order to cut down on costs.

Most food coops are organized on a neighborhood basis. Some work on a pre-order system, where members order and pay for the food a few days in advance of the pickup day. On the pickup day, a list for the following week is included with the order. Members generally work from two hours a month to two hours a week, depending upon the size and organization of the coop. Food can be purchased at wholesale prices and sold to members at a slight increase from wholesale, to cover the weekly costs of paper, supplies, and mistakes.

A second type of food coop is run more like a store. There are cash registers and the store is open six days a week. In this kind of coop, a nonrefundable membership fee is required. This money allows the coop to purchase freezers, coolers, and other equipment. The member then pays the wholesale price plus 10 percent. It's still a significant saving compared to the supermarket.

**How to form a coop.** Contact people in your area who might be interested. Put a notice up at the laundromat, the supermarket bulletin board, or a community building. Or ask among providers in your area. This is one area where a providers' support group can prove valuable.

A good resource book to read is *The Food Coop Handbook* by the Coop Handbook Collective (Houghton Mifflin, 1975). There are organizations in most states that compile information and act as clearinghouses for food coops in their areas. These offer helpful advice for groups forming coops. Often the larger organization will act as a buying service for a member food coop, for a fee that is below that of wholesalers. Look in the *People's Yellow Pages* or *Women's Yellow Pages,* which can be found in most bookstores. One organization to contact for some information is the Cooperative League of the U.S.A., 59 East Van Buren Street, Chicago, Illinois 60605.

**Some hints for buying food cooperatively:**
Watch to make sure the quantities you get from a wholesaler are exactly what you ordered, and that the quality is good.

Meat is ordered separately from a local meat wholesaler; since meat prices change frequently, the wholesaler must be willing to give you a fair price a week in advance. He must also be willing to deliver.

Cheese can usually be obtained from the same source as the meat. Cheese markets will sell wholesale only in wheels or blocks, so have enough people to use up a large chunk of cheese.

Bread is easily obtained at substantial reductions because it is usually ordered in quantities weekly. Check with your local bakery for reduced merchandise. If there is a large bakery near you, check to see if they have a thrift store for their products.

There are wholesale grocery stores scattered here and there throughout every state. It's worth it to see if a group of providers can arrange to purchase items here in bulk. Check for one near you.

## TALKING FROM EXPERIENCE:
### In the Providers' Own Words

Family day care providers themselves can often give the best help to each other simply by talking about the issues that come up. Here are some conversations and letters I have had from some of you in the last years.

### Problems with sharing.

My six children had some problems sharing both with each other and with my own baby girl. I had two children who were three years old, one who was two-and-a-half, and two who were almost six. The youngest were having a time fighting over toys and saying "mine" to anyone who approached the toy they were holding. The five-year-olds were enjoying playing with each other, but had a hard time understanding the concept of sharing.

I tried talking at first, and explaining. It helped, but the conflicts continued. Each still wanted the toy they were holding, even though they would nod that to share was a good thing. What to do? I am not easily frustrated, but this was getting on my nerves.

One afternoon while baking cookies for the children, I tried to think of a solution to our problem. Just then, the children all came into the house for an afternoon snack. I took the entire plate of cookies, sat down at the table, and started feasting on them—just like a Cookie Monster. When they asked me for one I replied, "No! I made these cookies and I did all the work and I'm not sharing any of them!" Such a startled look came over their faces! They just could not believe that a grownup would do such a selfish act. After a few seconds we all began to laugh at the silly thing I had done—they began to realize that sharing is for everyone and not just something children are made to do.

We sat down and talked about sharing. J. came up with the idea that we should make the turns shorter, and later have longer turns. O. and C. said that the younger children grab and should always say please, and S. said that she would try to remember to say please. And B. said anybody could ride his motorcycle. The children made great progress when they worked on the problem together with my help.

The children started bringing a sharing toy from their own houses just about every day. They had the privilege of showing it to everyone and telling them about it. A few days before Christmas we had a discussion about respecting one another's toys and taking care of them. When I observed the children sharing I always praised them and told them how happy I was. The preschooler's concept of sharing needs reinforcement from time to time, but most of the time they cooperated with each other.

In the past five months, their attitudes have really changed. Once in a while we will have a bad day, which can usually be attributed to fatigue or overexcitement. Sometimes the children just need an idea to expand their play: if we only have two airplanes and three children want to use them, I suggest that one child might be a fireman, in case the airport catches fire. The children are closer companions now, and I feel we have learned a great deal about sharing. Now we all enjoy each other and have fun!

### How to have a happier naptime.

Some of my kids nap well and some don't. It's hard for those ready to nap when others are making noise. I don't like to keep "sssssshhh"-ing them for the entire naptime. Here are some thoughts on the subject of napping.

Lots of factors determine how good or bad a particular naptime will be: weather, what happened before the nap, even things like what's going on at home and the phases of the moon affect children and their napping, in my opinion. There are always some naptimes that are no fun for anybody. The first thing I learned is that not every child will take a nap every day. *Rule Number 1: Be realistic in your expectations.*

Next, I started picking up on some techniques for insuring that children will have happy naptimes. Outdoor exercise is important. Children need to run off excess steam and the invigorating air makes everybody tired, even adults. I try to have my children out for at least a few minutes in the morning, and they seem to nap better.

I also have comfortable bedding for the children, and some have their own special blankets or soft quilts to lie on. If some children don't seem tired I give them a book to look at, and they can "rest." Sometimes a song or a back rub or rocking helps them to quiet down.

Important things I have learned include letting the children know what can and cannot go on during naptimes. It is a routine in my house, and we try to make it as pleasant as possible. When it is time to nap, it is time to be quiet. The children have come to know this. We also try to nap at the same time and in the same way every day so that everyone expects it.

I guess I believe that children need time to be quiet during the day (in order not to get overtired). I tell them that I get tired too, and need peace and quiet for a while. And that is true.

**The day when you've had it.**

The baby has been fussy, the two-year-old bites the three-year-old, the school-age children come home hot and asking, "What's there to do?" and then refuse to try anything you suggest, your own child is whining and clinging to your leg, and *you have just had it.* The day has not worked out the way you planned (who could have planned this?).

You really feel like walking out the door for some fresh air, alone. But you stay. And, by staying, you are actually showing the children a good thing. Everyone needs to learn to live comfortably with each other, even when they are feeling bad. They need to respect others and to live with themselves and with others. I sit down with my children and we talk about this. It takes a lot of self-control to hang in there on days like this, but it's an important thing to learn.

I have found ways to prevent this state of events from happening too often. I plan the day so that children have plenty of things to do, and can choose among them. I don't pull all of the toys out to play with, but leave a few and then bring them out when the children seem bored. Lots of times I plan something "special" for the day. Not anything elaborate, but something a bit different—like making cookies, reading a special book, a walk to the neighbors for a picnic afternoon snack, washing some dolls or a car on a hot day, setting up a lemonade stand (with homemade lemonade), and so on.

I try to balance activities: some quiet and some active. It helps, I find, to have a quiet activity going on before a routine such as lunch, nap, or going-home time.

It's good to lessen the time spent waiting. I have toys out when they first come, serve lunch within five minutes of when they sit down, and this seems to minimize the amount of poking at each other and scrambling on and off chairs.

If the children know what's coming next, they are better able to handle it. I give some warning when it will be time to go out or to pick up. I say something like, "When we have put away these scissors we will go on a walk." The children can then understand the sequence of events better. Or, I let my children know if there is a change in the schedule. If we go to the park, then I tell them there will be no nap today. But I don't tell them too far ahead of time, because even five minutes seems like forever for a child who is waiting.

This type of planning certainly makes my day run smoother.

## Stormy day outlet.

Want to know how to get the biggest stretch out of the smallest space? You will need two to three yards of half-inch elastic joined together firmly.

Begin with two children seated on the floor in a circle; each person takes hold of the elastic with both hands. Ask the children to watch you and to imitate what you do (to start). Raise your hands in front of you and stretch. Raise your arms over your head and stretch. Put one hand on your knee and one hand on your toe; work with the elastic behind your back. Go slowly, so that the children get a chance to feel the stretch in their bodies.

Let someone else be leader. While we do this, we talk about where your hands are in space. Are they over? Under? Behind? In front? How does that feel? Why doesn't this elastic break when you pull? What will break?

My preschoolers and the after-school children love this stretching. The toddlers will pull the elastic if you give each of them a piece, so they are part of it.

## A child who clings.

I have a little boy who was overly dependent on me. J. wore me out with asking "What is there to do?" and when I suggested something, he would say, "I will do it if you will do it with me." He would follow behind me and ask endless questions geared to getting attention more than information. When I sat down to read a story, J. would be the first to climb into my lap. He would scream if any of the other children tried to climb up too. I really liked J., but was beginning to dread seeing him come in the morning, knowing that I would have to spend a whole day with his clinging behavior.

At first I really tried to understand his behavior. Often a child will do this when they haven't been with you for a long time and the problem will resolve itself as the child becomes more secure in your home. J. had been with me for five months and I thought he felt good about being in my home. There were no big changes in my home or his that I knew of. The day care children had remained the same and J. played well with all of them.

Puzzled, I asked his mother what might be happening at home that would affect him. She couldn't think of anything she had noticed except a bit more whining. She did say that she felt they had very little time to spend together. By the time they got home, had dinner and a bath, and got ready for a story and bed, that left maybe one hour at the most for just relaxing together.

We both thought J. might be reacting to not enough time with just one adult and was demanding more during the daytime with me because he couldn't at night. He also just might have been going through a stage of dependency. Often children will alternate times of being dependent with times of being very independent.

What could his mother and I do to try to help J.? I tried to give him attention in a friendly, approving way, and at the same time lessen his dependency on me. When J. asked to build a farm for his rubber animals with me, I would point out that he could build a good farm by himself with some empty cereal cartons for the barns. I would sit with J. for a while as he started to build and then move away, but reassure him that I would be nearby. I praised him while he worked, and when he was done I commented on how well he could build by himself. I also brought out activities that J. enjoyed. This helped him to get involved in playing by himself. There were some moments during the day when he needed to sit in my lap, and this was allowed. When he seemed to have had enough, he would crawl back down and I would suggest a favorite activity for him to start.

After a period of weeks, he seemed to have lost some of the clinging behavior and was much happier. So was I. I guess one thing I realized afterward was that children are after all very small and dependent on adults. We try to foster independence, but still need to realize that it is hard for them to be away from their parent(s) all day, and that this will occasionally wear on them and show in their behavior.

## Your own child and the day care children.

Why is it always (or so it seems) your own child that has the hardest time sharing and the worst tantrums? Sometimes you may find it easier to soothe another child than your own on the day that yours is having a hard time coping with life. I have found that my own children have a big adjustment to the day care service I provide for others' children. I often have to spend a little more time thinking how to make my own child feel secure and happy with my job. The following techniques have helped me and my preschooler with the adjustment to day care children:

• Let your child help prepare for the activities for the day care children. For instance, take your child to the store and let him/her help pick out apples for the applesauce you plan to make with the others. This helps him feel a part of the job and a little special. It also prepares him for the day's activities.

• Show a little extra affection and attention at times he seems to need it. The other children will accept this.

• Give your child a break from the day care home whenever possible. If a friend or grandparent asks my child to go on a special outing, I agree. It is usually a time for the child to get a little extra attention with just one adult.

• Some days I just have to be prepared for my child to have a hard time sharing me and his home. I have to realize that it is a lot to ask a young child to do and understand there will be some difficult times.

**"A day in the life" of one provider.** Although there are no two days alike, it's a comfort to know what's coming next. It is important to children, also, to know what is going to happen in the family day care home. They come to depend on a certain order of the day. Simple routines of eating, sleeping, playing, and such are the basic groundwork around which your day may evolve.

Here's a sketch of a day in the life of a family day care provider—one woman's typical routine. Some providers get up at 5 or 6 a.m. and the last children often don't leave until late in the evenings.

*7 a.m.:* Rise and awaken my son for school; prepare breakfast and hurry my son off; feed the baby and family.

*8 a.m.:* Dress the other children in my family.

*9 a.m.:* Clean kitchen, dishes, straighten up as time permits; put my baby down for morning nap; eat my breakfast and check the morning paper.

*9:15 a.m.:* M. (3½) arrives and plays with my daughter in playhouse with dolls; I make beds and straighten up bedrooms.

*10 a.m.:* Morning snack; children play with playdough or clay.

*11 a.m.:* Baby is awake and fed; girls watch "Sesame Street"; I prepare lunch.

*11:45 a.m.:* My son returns from school; the children have lunch together while I feed the baby.

*12:15 p.m.:* Older children play together; I clean up the baby and then the kitchen.

*12:30 p.m.:* I put the baby down for a nap and eat lunch.

*1:30 p.m.:* C. (10 months) arrives.

*2 p.m.:* M. and my daughter go for a nap (half the time M. doesn't nap); C. has a bottle.

*2:30 p.m.:* C. goes for a nap; baby wakes up; son goes outside to play with friends; I play with baby, talk and read with my own children, or we do a project (painting, pasting); I prepare the dinner in advance and keep it warm.

*4:30 p.m.:* C. and M. awaken from nap; C. has a bottle; older children watch "Sesame Street" while I play with C. and the baby.

*5:30 p.m.:* C. and M. leave; my husband arrives; dinner is ready to be put on the table.

*6 p.m.:* Baths and teeth-brushing for my children.

*6:30 p.m.:* My children watch favorite T.V. programs; husband and I clean up kitchen and talk.

*7 p.m.:* Bedtime for all three children.

This schedule varies sometimes; my older boy goes out to play and the other children take naps at the same time. If that happens, I grab a snooze myself.

# 10. RESOURCES FOR PROVIDERS

## READING MATERIAL

**Magazines.** Here are a few magazines that have information on child development, parenthood, and day care.

- *Day Care and Early Childhood Education,* 92 Fifth Avenue, New York, New York 10011. This is a fairly new bimonthly magazine with much good information concerning family day care as well as other forms of child care. There is a column specifically about activities for infants, toddlers, and preschoolers.
- *Parent's Magazine,* Parents Institute, Bergenfield, New Jersey 07621. Published monthly by the Parents Institute, this contains articles on child rearing, activities for children of different ages, and almost anything that concerns parents and families.

- *Redbook Magazine,* Box 2036, Rock Island, Illinois 61206. This monthly magazine has columns by such people as Dr. Spock, Dr. Brazelton, and Margaret Mead, in which many issues are discussed involving child care and development and parenthood.

**Government publications.** The U.S. Government Printing Office publishes numerous booklets on child care, child development, and parenthood. You can get any of them at no charge by writing to: U.S. Government Printing Office, Washington, D.C. 20402.

- *Caring for Children* series, by Lois Murphy and Ethel Leeper. These include:
    *The Ways Children Learn*
    *More Than a Teacher*
    *Preparing for Change*
    *Away from Bedlam*
    *The Vulnerable Child*
- *A Guide for Parents* series, including:
    *Talk with Baby* (No. 361)
    *Babies Look and Learn* (No. 362)
    *Playing Games with Baby* (No. 425)
    *Home Play and Play Equipment* (No. 238)
- *Publications for Parents* series, including:
    *Infant Care* (DHEW [OCD] No. 73-15)
    *Your Child from 1 to 3* (No. 413)
    *Your Child from 3 to 4* (No. 446)
    *Your Child from 1 to 6* (No. 30-1)
    *Your Child from 6 to 12* (No. 324)

There are also some government publications on day care and family day care in particular. These are:

- *Day Care for Your Child in a Family Home* (no. 411)
- *Day Care for Other People's Children in Your Home* (No. 412)
- *What Is Good Day Care?* (OCD No. 72-43)
- *Day Care Services: Why? What? Where? When? How?* (No. 426)

- *Bibliography of Home-Based Child Development Program Resources* (OCD No. 74-1967)

To get a complete publications list before you order, write for OCD No. 72-22 at:

Office of Child Development
U.S. Department of Health, Education, and Welfare
P.O. Box 1182
Washington, D.C. 20013

The Massachusetts Department of Mental Health has produced some excellent materials for helping disabled children. Two publications that suggest activities for children with special needs are:

- *Home Stimulation,* for young, developmentally disabled children.
- *Exploring Materials,* for use with your young child with special needs.

Write to: Commonwealth Mental Health Foundation, 4 Marlboro Road, Lexington, Massachusetts 02173.

**Other sources for booklets.** In addition to the government publications discussed above, there are many useful pamphlets put out by private industry or associations of various kinds. What follows is a list of many I have found worth sending for, together with the appropriate addresses.

- Human Relations Aids
  419 Park Avenue South
  New York, New York 10016

    *Destructiveness*
    *Bed-Wetting*
    *School*
    *Fear*
    *Temper*
    *The Only Child*
    *Building Self-Confidence*
    *Discipline*

*Baby Talk*
*Stuttering*
*Sex*
*Thumbsucking*

- Institute of Child and Family Development
University of North Carolina
Greensboro, North Carolina 27412

    Write for a catalog of the inexpensive materials
    prepared by this group. They include:
    *Discipline: The Secret Heart of Child Care,* by
        M. E. Keister (1972)
    *What Parents Should Look For ... Special*
        *Provisions for Infants and Toddlers*
        (UNC-G)

- Johnson & Johnson, Inc.
Consumer Service Department
New Brunswick, New Jersey 08903

    *Keeping Baby Clean*
    *Chart: How a Baby Grows*
    *When Baby Is Ill*
    *Baby's Eating and Sleeping Habits*
    *A Safer World for Babies and Toddlers*

- The National Association for Mental Health, Inc.
10 Columbus Circle
New York, New York 10019

    *What the Early Child Needs*

- The Press
Case Western Reserve University
10910 Euclid Avenue
Cleveland, Ohio 44106

    *Kids Copy Their Parents*
    *Keep Babies Busy*

- Publications
  205 Whitten Hall
  University of Missouri
  Columbia, Missouri 65201

    *Isn't It Wonderful How Babies Learn?*

- Ross Laboratories
  Columbus, Ohio 43216

    *Your Children and Discipline*
    *Your Children's Quarrels*
    *Your Children's Fears*
    *Your Child's Appetite*
    *Developing Toilet Habits*
    *The Phenomena of Early Development*

- Science Research Association
  259 East Erie Street
  Chicago, Illinois 60604

    *Some Special Problems of Children Aged 2 to 5,*
    by Nina Ridenour
    *Behavior: The Unspoken Language of Children,* by Child Study Association (Third
    Printing, 1973)

Note: Most of these pamphlets are even more inexpensive in bulk; do you know other providers who might be interested if you decide to order them?

**Especially on family day care.**

- Child Care Resource Center
  123 Mount Auburn Street
  Cambridge, Massachusetts 02138
    *A Family Day Care Study.* A study of family day care systems in Massachusetts.

- Audio-Visual Library Service
  University of Minnesota
  3300 University Avenue, S.E.
  Minneapolis, Minnesota 55414
    *Family Day Care: A Self-Portrait.* This is a pictorial essay published by the Ramsey County Family Day Care Training Project in Minnesota in 1973-1974.

- Day Care and Child Development Council of America (DCCDCA)
  1401 K Street, N.W.
  Washington, D.C.
    *I'm Not Just a Sitter*

- Demonstration and Research Center for Early Education (Darcee)
  Publication Office
  George Peabody College for Teachers
  Box 151
  Nashville, Tennessee 37203
    *A Handbook for Family Day Care Workers.* This booklet was produced in December 1971 by the DARCEE Family Day Care Project and provides some excellent information about the importance of family day care providers in the early learning of young children.

- Superintendent of Documents
  Government Printing Office
  Washington, D.C. 20402
    *Family Day Care No. 9* (Stock No. 1791-00188). This is number 9 in a series on child care, published by the Office of Child Development of the U.S. Department of Health, Education, and Welfare. There are sections on how to set up a home for family day care, working with parents, record-keeping, and resources.

- Child Development Training Program
  166 Old Main

Wayne State University
Detroit, Michigan 48202
> *Handbook for Home Care of Children.* This booklet
> was prepared by a group of family day care providers
> in a course at Wayne State University as part of that
> university's Child Development Training Program in
> 1971.

- EID Associates, Inc.
  2520 South State Street
  Salt Lake City, Utah 84115
  > *Guide for Family Day Care.* A guide for providers,
  > including sections on getting started, record-
  > keeping, discipline, and community resources.

- *Family Day Care: A Practical Guide for Parents, Caregivers, and Professionals,* by Alice H. Collins and Enice
  L. Watson (Beacon Press, 1976)


**Books on child development**

- *Black Child Care: How To Bring Up a Healthy Black
  Child in America,* by James Comer and Alvin F.
  Pouissant (Pocket Books, 1976)
  Pouissant (Pocket Books, 1976). This is probably the first
  comprehensive approach to the rearing of a black child in
  America. It includes questions and answers about family
  planning, prenatal cares, infancy, preschool years, and
  puberty.

- *Infants and Mothers,* by T. Berry Brazelton (Dell, 1972).
  A descriptive study of three general types of babies in
  their first year, and their mothers, by a very sensitive
  pediatrician. Dr. Brazelton has also written *Toddlers and
  Parents* (Dell, 1976).

- *The Magic Years,* by Selma Fraiberg (Scribner, 1968). An
  informative book about understanding and handling the
  problems of early childhood.

## ORGANIZATIONS AND AGENCIES CONCERNED WITH CHILDREN

There are many organizations throughout the country that are concerned with the needs of young children. Most publish information in the form of articles, pamphlets, or periodicals. You can be a member (for a price) and receive information regularly, or you can send off for whatever information specifically interests you. Here are only a few:

- Association for Childhood Education International (ACEI)
  3615 Wisconsin Avenue, N.W.
  Washington, D.C.
  This association is concerned with the education of young children. It has many materials on nursery school and kindergarten, as well as bulletins, portfolios, papers, and books. *Childhood Education* is the journal it publishes.

- Black Child Development Institute
  1028 Connecticut Avenue N.W.
  Washington, D.C. 20036

- Child Welfare League of America
  67 Irving Place
  New York, New York 10022
  This organization is involved in all aspects of child welfare, day care services, adoption, and foster family care. It has materials, plus a monthly periodical called *Child Welfare.*

- Day Care and Child Development Council of America, Inc.
  1012 14th Street N.W.
  Washington, D.C. 20005
  This council aims "to promote the development of a locally controlled, publicly supported, universally available child-care system through public education, social action, and assistance to local committees, the child, the

family, and the community." It offers a great selection of materials on day care and child development, and a special membership fee for family day care providers. Publications include *Voice for Children* and *Family Day Care Provider*.

• National Association for the Education of Young Children (NAEYC)
1834 Connecticut Avenue N.W.
Washington, D.C. 20009
This association is interested in the education of young children. It holds conferences both nationally and locally throughout the year, and has a large supply of materials on early childhood education. Check in your area for a local affiliate of this organization. It publishes *Young Children* bimonthly.

• National Organization for Women
Task Force on Child Care
45 Newbury Street
Boston, Massachusetts 02116

• State Department of Mental Health
(Look in the yellow pages for the address.)
There are usually several mental health regions in each state, coordinating a variety of services. These might include counseling and evaluation for adults, children, couples, and families; in-patient psychiatric care; 24-hour emergency service; retardation facilities; community clinical nursery schools; day care for disturbed and retarded people; and services for geriatric care, drug abuse, and alcoholism. For specific information about services near you, call your regional or area office.

• State Department of Public Health
(Look in the yellow pages for the address.)
Departments of public health offer a wide range of services. These include hearing and vision clinics (especially for preschoolers); dental screening; pediatric examinations; immunizations; sickle-cell anemia testing;

tuberculosis testing; and well baby clinics. Services for crippled children are also offered. Well baby clinics provide free medical and nursing services to children from birth to six years, with the focus on illness *prevention* and child development.

- Child Care Resource Center, Inc.
  Cambridge Street
  Cambridge, Mass.
      This center has a wealth of materials and information for those concerned with child care in its many aspects.

- Children in Hospitals
  31 Wilshire Park
  Needham, Massachusetts 02192
      This organization of persons concerned with children in hospitals provides useful material about issues that arise when children are hospitalized, including information on the rights of parents and children. Look for a similar organization in your area.

- Action for Children's Television (ACT)
  46 Austin Street
  Newtonville, Massachusetts 02160
      ACT is a national organization to monitor and improve the quality of children's television programming and to eliminate offensive advertising. It publishes a newsletter, and interested persons are invited to join the group.

- The Children's Defense Fund
  1746 Cambridge Street
  Cambridge, Massachusetts 02138
      This is a national organization concerned with the rights of children.

Note: For extensive listings of resources for the health, education, and welfare of children, check the *People's Yellow Pages* or the *Parent's Yellow Pages,* by the Princeton Center for Infancy (Anchor Books, 1978).

## SUGGESTED BOOKS FOR CHILDREN

Whether you get your children's books at the library, the bookstore, or your neighbor's garage sale, it's always helpful to know which are the all-time favorites. Some of the books listed here will be out of print, so you may not be able to buy them new. But all are well worth keeping your eyes open for. For purposes of length, I am only including the authors and titles of these books (not the publishing information); your librarian can help you locate them and can also point out other good books.

**For very young children.** Cloth books that can be washed after a lot of handling are very practical. Some of these include *Baby's First Book, Baby's Things, Baby's Pets,* and Dorothy Kunhardt's classic *Pat the Bunny.* Other favorites are:

> Marjorie Flack:
>> *Angus and the Cat*
>> *Angus Lost*
>> *Wait for William*
> Arthur Gregor, *Animal Babies*
> Ezra Jack Keats:
>> *The Snowy Day*
>> *Whistle for Willie*
> Ruth Krauss, *The Carrot Seed*
> Ethel Wright, *Saturday Walk*
> Blanch F. Wright, *The Real Mother Goose*

**For preschool children.** There is a rich variety of excellent books to read aloud to your three to five year olds.

> Joan Anglund, *A Friend Is Someone Who Likes You*
> Ludwig Bemelmans:
>> *Madeline*
>> *Madeline and the Bad Hat*
>> *Madeline and the Gypsies*
>> *Madeline in London*
>> *Madeline's Rescue*
>> *The City Noisy Book*
>> *Madeline's Rescue*

Margaret W. Brown:
  *The City Noisy Book*
  *The Country Noisy Book*
  *The Dead Bird*
  *Goodnight Moon*
  *The Runaway Bunny*
Virginia L. Burton:
  *Katy and the Big Snow*
  *The Little House*
  *Mike Mulligan and His Steam Shovel*
James Daugherty, *Andy and the Lion*
Marie Hall Ets, *Just Me*
Marjorie Flack:
  *Ask Mr. Bear*
  *The Story About Ping*
  *Angus and the Cat*
  *Angus Lost*
Don Freeman:
  *Corduroy*
  *Dandelion*
Wanda Gag, *Millions of Cats*
Crockett Johnson, *Harold and the Purple Crayon*
Ruth Krauss, *Bears*
Lois Lenski:
  *I Like Winter*
  *The Little Auto*
  *The Little Airplane*
  *Papa Small*
Leo Lionel, *Inch by Inch*
Robert McCloskey:
  *Blueberries for Sal*
  *Make Way for Ducklings*
  *One Morning in Maine*
Else H. Minarik:
  *Little Bear*
  *Little Bear's Visit*
  *Father Bear Comes Home*
Bruno Munari, *Bruno Munari's ABC*

Clare Newberry, *T-Bone, the Baby-Sitter*
Watty Piper, *The Little Engine That Could*
Beatrix Potter, *The Tale of Peter Rabbit*
Alvin Tresselt:
  *Rain Drop Splash*
  *White Snow, Bright Snow*
Bernard Waber, *The House on East Eighty-Eighth St.*
Taro Yashima, *Umbrella*
Charlotte Zolotow, *Storm Book*
H. A. Rey, *Curious George,* and others
Richard Scarry, *Great Big Car and Truck Book*
Julian Scheer, *Rain Makes Applesauce*
Herman Schneider and Nina Schneider, *How Big Is*
Herman and Nina Schneider, *How Big Is Big?*
Maurice Sendak:
  *In the Night Kitchen*
  *Where the Wild Things Are*
Esphyr Slobodkina, *Caps for Sale*

**For the school-age child.** Ask the librarian to help your six to nine year olds find books they might like. Here are a few standard ones.

Rebecca Caudill,
  *Did You Carry the Flag Today, Charley?*
Elizabeth Guilfoile, *Nobody Listens to Andrew*
Robert McCloskey:
  *Homer Price*
  *Lentil*
Lynd Ward, *The Biggest Bear*
E. B. White:
  *Charlotte's Web*
  *Stuart Little*
  *The Trumpet of the Swan*
Laura Ingalls Wilder:
  *Little House in the Big Woods*
  *Little House on the Prairie*
  *Farmer Boy*
  *On the Banks of Plum Creek*
Herbert S. Zim, *Dinosaurs*

## RESOURCES FOR MUSIC ACTIVITIES

**Suggestions for songbooks.** Here are a few books of songs that are favorites in many homes.

> Margaret Boni, *The Fireside Book of Folk Songs*
> Ethel Crowninshield, *Stories That Sing*
> Beatrice Landeck, *Songs To Grow On*
> Ruth Crawford Seeger,
> *American Folk Songs for Children*
> Marlo Thomas, *Free To Be . . . You and Me*

**Records for singing and listening.** Children love to listen to folk songs and sing along to records. Here are a few.

> Woodie Guthrie:
> *Songs to Grow On: Nursery Days*
> *Songs To Grow On: School Days*
> *Songs To Grow On for Mother and Children*
> *This Land Is Your Land*
> Burl Ives,
> *Little White Duck and Other Children's Favorites*
> Pete Seeger:
> *American Folk Songs for Children*
> *Birds, Beasts, Bugs, and Little Fishes*
> *Abiyoyo and Other Story Songs for Children*
> Children's Television Workshop,
> *Sesame Street, Rubber Duckie, and Other Songs*

Here are some suggested lullaby songs for listening and falling asleep to:

> Nancy Rowen, *Lullabies and Other Children's Songs*
> Marilyn Horne and Richard Robinson,
> *Lullabies from Round the World*

**Records for rhythms and movement.**

*A Visit to My Little Friend* (Children's Record Guild)
*Calypso Songs for Children* (Columbia)
*Doing the Hokey Pokey* (Cricket)
*Let's Play a Musical Game and Others* (Columbia)
*Music of the Sioux and the Navajo* (Ethnic Folkways)
Ella Jenkins, *Rhythms of Childhood* (Folkways)
*Spanish Dances* (Folkways)
*Walk, Skip, Gallop, Run, Tiptoe* (Children's Record Guild)
Ella Jenkins, *You'll Sing a Song, I'll Sing a Song* (Folkways)

**Where to get records.** Here are a few record companies that offer a number of records for children. They will send you catalogs upon request.

Columbia Children's Record Library
CBS  Inc.
15 West 52 Street
New York, NY 10036

Folkways
701 Seventh Avenue
New York, NY 10036

Weston Woods Studios
Weston, CT

Children's Book and Music Center
2858 West Pico Boulevard
Los Angeles, CA 90006
(This is a book and record store on the West Coast that offers a large selection of records and books. A catalog is available.)

**APPENDIX A: Sample Registration Form for a Child in Your Care**

Child: _____ Birthdate: _____

Mother: _____
       (name)      (address)     (phone)

       _____
       (place of employment)  (address)    (phone)

Father: _____
       (name)      (address)     (phone)

       _____
       (place of employment)  (address)    (phone)

If parents are not available, nearest friend or relative to contact in case of an emergency:

Name: _____ Address: _____ Phone: _____

Child's doctor: _____
       (name)      (phone)

       _____
       (address)  (hospital to use in an emergency)

Date child started day care in this home: _____

Date child ended day care in this home: _____

**APPENDIX B**

## MEDICAL EMERGENCY STATEMENT

I hereby give permission for _____
                                                    *Provider's Name*
to call a physician, secure necessary medical care (including
the administration of anaesthesia if surgery is advised by a
physician), and to otherwise act in my behalf in order to
protect my child when I cannot be reached and/or when
delay would be dangerous in case of illness or accident.


_____
                    *Signature of Parent or Guardian*


_____
                                    *Date*

**APPENDIX C: Sample Letter to Parents of Children Starting in Your Home**

Dear _____

    It sure was nice meeting you and your child. Prices are high these days and day care is no exception; to keep up with the times, I charge $_____ per week. It helps me keep my records straight if everyone pays at about the same time, on the _____ of the week (month).

    This fee includes snacks in the morning and afternoon, a hot meal from my kitchen at noon (or a beverage with a bag lunch), materials for creating things, lots of tender loving care, and just about anything else that comes up.

    If we go on a special trip to the zoo or elsewhere, I ask that you supply a small amount of money for admission and perhaps for some peanuts for the elephants.

    You may drop your child at _____ a.m. and, since I need to fix my own family their dinner in the evening, I would appreciate it if you picked your child up no later than _____ p.m.

    Since young children have the habit of needing a change of clothes during the day, please supply me with a complete change so that I am prepared.

    I feel strongly about knowing the people who come to pick your child up. As I understand it, only the following persons are okay for doing this: (name, address, phone number, and relationship).

    Thank you, and I hope to be seeing you often at my home.

                          Sincerely,

## APPENDIX D: Weekly Expense Form

| FOOD: | Cost | | UTILITIES: | Cost |
|---|---|---|---|---|
| Bread | $ | | Water | $ |
| Cereal | $ | | Electricity | $ |
| Meat | $ | | Gas | $ |
| Cheese | $ | | Rent or mortgage | $ |
| Soup | $ | | Telephone | $ |
| Juice | $ | | Other | $ |
| Milk | $ | | Total | $ |
| Eggs | $ | | | |
| Butter | $ | | DEPRECIATION: | |
| Mayonnaise | $ | | | |
| Fruit | $ | | House | $ |
| Vegetables | $ | | Renovations | $ |
| Other | $ | | Washing machine | $ |
| Total: | $ | | Refrigerator | $ |
| | | | Stove | $ |
| HOUSEHOLD: | | | Furnace | $ |
| | | | Other | $ |
| Toilet paper | $ | | Total | $ |
| Paper towels | $ | | | |
| Soap | $ | | PLAY MATERIALS OR EQUIPMENT | |
| Dish detergent | $ | | List items purchased: | |
| Disposable diapers | $ | | _____ | $ |
| Napkins, cups, | | | _____ | $ |
| dishes | $ | | Total | $ |
| Cloth, towels | $ | | | |
| Other | $ | | OTHER COSTS: | |
| Total | $ | | | |
| | | | Travel | $ |
| | | | Laundry, cleaning | $ |
| | | | Repairs | $ |
| | | | Total | $ |

## APPENDIX E: Monthly Expense Form

AMOUNT SPENT PER MONTH ON DAY CARE EXPENSES

|  | January | February | March | April | (etc.) |
|---|---|---|---|---|---|
| Food: | | | | | |
| Household: | | | | | |
| Educational Equipment: | | | | | |
| Furnishings: | | | | | |
| First Aid, Medicines: | | | | | |
| Maintenance, Repair: | | | | | |
| Insurance: | | | | | |
| Salaries | | | | | |
|   Helper No. 1: | | | | | |
|   Helper No. 2: | | | | | |
| Amortization: | | | | | |
| Mortgage: | | | | | |
| Heat: | | | | | |
| Electricity: | | | | | |
| Telephone: | | | | | |
| Transportation: | | | | | |

## APPENDIX F: Income Form

JANUARY–JUNE 198__

| Child's Name | January | | | | February | | | | March |
|---|---|---|---|---|---|---|---|---|---|
| | 4th | 11th | 18th | 25th | 1st | 8th | 15th | 22nd | 1st |
| Mary Jones | $20 | $20 | $20 | $20 | — | — | — | — | — |
| John O'Leary | $15 | $15 | $ 9 | $15 | — | — | — | — | — |
| Travis Scott | $20 | $20 | $20 | 0 | — | — | — | — | — |

## APPENDIX G: Attendance Form

### MONTH:

### Hours Attended Day Care

| Child's Name | 1 | 2 | 3 | 4 | 5 | 6 | 7 | 8 | 9 | 10 | 11 | 12 | ... 31 |
|---|---|---|---|---|---|---|---|---|---|---|---|---|---|
| Mary Jones | 0 | 4 | 4 | 4 | 4 | 4 | 0 | | | | | | |
| John O'Leary | 0 | 9 | 9 | 9 | 9 | 9 | 0 | | | | | | |
| Travis Scott | 0 | 8 | 8 | 8 | 8 | 9 | 0 | | | | | | |

# APPENDIX H: Income Tax Form for Family Day Care Provider

| SCHEDULE C (Form 1040) | **Profit or (Loss) From Business or Profession** | 1979 |
|---|---|---|

**SCHEDULE C (Form 1040)**
Department of the Treasury
Internal Revenue Service

**Profit or (Loss) From Business or Profession**
(Sole Proprietorship)
Partnerships, Joint Ventures, etc., Must File Form 1065.
► Attach to Form 1040 or Form 1041.  ► See Instructions for Schedule C (Form 1040).

**19 79**
09

Name of proprietor | Social security number of proprietor

**A** Main business activity (see Instructions) ► _____ ; product ► _____

**B** Business name ► _____     **C** Employer identification number

**D** Business address (number and street) ► _____
City, State and Zip Code ►

**E** Accounting method: (1) ☐ Cash  (2) ☐ Accrual  (3) ☐ Other (specify) ► _____     **C**

**F** Method(s) used to value closing inventory:
(1) ☐ Cost  (2) ☐ Lower of cost or market  (3) ☐ Other (if other, attach explanation)

|  | Yes | No |
|---|---|---|
| **G** Was there any major change in determining quantities, costs, or valuations between opening and closing inventory? . . If "Yes," attach explanation. | | |
| **H** Did you deduct expenses for an office in your home? . . . . . . . . . . . . . . . . . . . | | |
| **I** Did you elect to claim amortization (under section 191) or depreciation (under section 167(o)) for a rehabilitated certified historic structure (see Instructions)? . . . . . . . . . . . . . . . . . (Amortizable basis (see Instructions) ►          ) | | |

**Part I    Income**

| | | |
|---|---|---|
| 1 a Gross receipts or sales . . . . . . . . | 1a | |
| b Returns and allowances . . . . . . . . | 1b | |
| c Balance (subtract line 1b from line 1a) . . . . . . . . . . . . . . . . | 1c | |
| 2 Cost of goods sold and/or operations (Schedule C–1, line 8) . . . . . . . . . . . | 2 | |
| 3 Gross profit (subtract line 2 from line 1c) . . . . . . . . . . . . . . . . . | 3 | |
| 4 Other income (attach schedule) . . . . . . . . . . . . . . . . . . . . | 4 | |
| 5 Total income (add lines 3 and 4) . . . . . . . . . . . . . . . . . . ► | 5 | |

**Part II    Deductions**

| | | |
|---|---|---|
| 6 Advertising . . . . . . . . | 31 a Wages . . | |
| 7 Amortization . . . . . . . | b Jobs credit | |
| 8 Bad debts from sales or services . | c WIN credit | |
| 9 Bank charges . . . . . . . | d Total credits | |
| 10 Car and truck expenses . . . . | e Subtract line 31d from 31a . | |
| 11 Commissions . . . . . . . | 32 Other expenses (specify): | |
| 12 Depletion . . . . . . . . | a | |
| 13 Depreciation (explain in Schedule C–2) . | b | |
| 14 Dues and publications . . . . | c | |
| 15 Employee benefit programs . . | d | |
| 16 Freight (not included on Schedule C–1) . | e | |
| 17 Insurance . . . . . . . . | f | |
| 18 Interest on business indebtedness | g | |
| 19 Laundry and cleaning . . . . | h | |
| 20 Legal and professional services . | i | |
| 21 Office supplies . . . . . . | j | |
| 22 Pension and profit-sharing plans . | k | |
| 23 Postage . . . . . . . . . | l | |
| 24 Rent on business property . . . | m | |
| 25 Repairs . . . . . . . . . | n | |
| 26 Supplies (not included on Schedule C–1) . | o | |
| 27 Taxes . . . . . . . . . . | p | |
| 28 Telephone . . . . . . . . | q | |
| 29 Travel and entertainment . . . | r | |
| 30 Utilities . . . . . . . . . | s | |

| | |
|---|---|
| 33 Total deductions (add amounts in columns for lines 6 through 32s) . . . . . . . . . . ► | 33 |
| 34 Net profit or (loss) (subtract line 33 from line 5). If a profit, enter on Form 1040, line 13, and on Schedule SE, Part II, line 5a (or Form 1041, line 6). If a loss, go on to line 35 . . . . . | 34 |

35 If you have a loss, do you have amounts for which you are not "at risk" in this business (see Instructions)? . . ☐ Yes  ☐ No

# INDEX

Accident insurance, 91. *See also*
  Emergencies
Adjustment period with new child, 94
Adult education, 46–47
After-school care, 32–33
Airports, visiting with children, 37–38
Allergies, of children, 48, 95
Applesauce, making, 60
Aquariums, visiting with children, 38
Arboretums, visiting with children, 38
Art for preschoolers, 23–27
Assistance
  during field trips, 79
  for providers, 43–46
Association, family day care, 4
Audubon Society, visiting with children,
  38
Automobile insurance, 91

Baby food, 52–55
  making, 51–52, 71
Babysitters, differences from, 5
Back-up provider, 43
Bakeries, visiting with children, 38
Banana bread, recipe for, 58–59
Bathtub safety, 74
Beef stew, for babies, 53–54
Bicycle
  safety, 80
  seats, for children, 80
Books
  for babies, 122
  of ideas for providers, 35–36
  making your own, 34, 67
  nonsexist children's, 35
  reading, to children, 34–35, 122–25
  for school-age children, 124
  for toddlers, 22, 122–24
Buddy system, for providers, 45
Building
  activities for children, 12–13, 28–30, 33
  free materials for, 40–42
Butter, making, 59

Car seats, for children, 80–81
Chicken and rice stew, for babies, 54

Chicken soup, recipe for, 57
Child abuse
  agencies dealing with, 83
  reporting, 82
  resources for parents, 82–83
  warning signs of, 81–82
Child development, 17
  courses in, 44, 45–46
  publications on, 112–18
  stages of, 18
Child neglect. *See* Child abuse
Children's services, state offices for, 7
Choking, 74
Clay
  baker's, how to make, 27
  modeling with, 26–27, 33
  peanut butter, how to make, 27
  *See also* Playdough
Cleaning up, with children, 10, 12
Clinging in children, 108–9
Construction sites, visiting with children,
  38
Cooking, with children, 67–68
Crayons, 25
  soap, 26

Deductions, tax
  for educational expenses, 87
  for food costs, 86–87, 130, 131
  for supplies, 85–86, 130, 131
  for use of home, 87–90
Department of public health, 7
Department of public welfare, 7
Disasters, learning from, 15–16
Discipline
  discussing, with parents, 92, 93
  reference books on, 99, 112–18
  spanking as form of, 99
Dramatic play, 22–23, 33

Eating habits, 48–49, 93
Educational resources, 46–47
Emergencies
  information from parents about, 94
  procedures for, 73
  reference books on, 76–79
  telephone numbers for, 73

Peanut butter, making, 59-60
Pick-up of child, 96-97, 99-100
Picnics, with children, 39
Plants, activities with, 13-15, 33
Playdough, how to make, 26-27
Poison, 74, 75, 76
  control center, 77-78
  emergency procedures for, 76
  information on, 77-78
Poisonous plants, 78
Police stations, visiting with children, 39
Popcorn, 60
Post offices, visiting with children, 39
Preschoolers, activities for, 22-32
Provider's children, 109-10
Publications useful to providers, 112-118
Pudding, making, 60

Reading to children, 34-35
Record keeping
  of data on children, 127, 128, 129, 132
  filing systems for, 84, 87
  for provider's expenses, 130, 131
  for tax purposes, 85-91, 130, 131, 133
Records for children, 126
Referral, 3
Registration. *See* Licensing
Registration form for children in
  provider's care, 127
Role model, provider as, 16

Safety, 7, 67-68
  bicycle, 80
  car, 80-81
  courses in, 46
  electrical, 75
  precautions in the home, 73-76
Salary, 3
Schedules
  of arrival and pick-up times, 96, 99-100
  sample of provider's, 110-11
  for vacation, 96
Scrounging for materials, 40-43
Separation
  child's anxiety about, 92-93, 98
  parents' anxiety about, 97-98

Sharing, problems with, 104-5
Snacks, 49-51
  for babies, 54-55
  recipes for, 55, 61-62
Snow
  activities with, 27-28
  making ice cream from, 61
Soap crayons, how to make, 26
Social Security taxes, 90
Spanking. *See* Discipline
Support groups, 4, 101-2

Table setting, with children, 12
Taxes
  information about, 90
  Social Security, 90
  work sheet for, 133
Television for children, 121
Toddlers
  activities for, 10, 20-22
  toys for, 20-21
Toilet training
  discussing, with parents, 93, 98
  publications about, 116
Tools, for children, 28
Toys
  appropriate, at different stages, 18
  dangerous, 78-79, 102
  discussing, with parents, 93
  for infants, 19
  for toddlers, 20-21
Training, 3
Triwall, 13
Tuberculosis test, 7

Vacation
  policy during, 96
  for provider, 43, 96
Vegetable soup, recipe for, 56-57
Volunteer help for providers, 44

Water, activities with, 11
Woodworking, 28

*Yellow Pages of Learning,* 40

Zoos, visiting with children, 39-40